AMERICAN NATURE GUIDES
ROCKS AND MINERALS

AMERICAN NATURE GUIDES
ROCKS AND MINERALS

MICHAEL O'DONOGHUE

GALLERY BOOKS
An Imprint of W. H. Smith Publishers Inc.
112 Madison Avenue
New York City 10016

This edition first published in the United States 1990 by
Gallery Books, an imprint of W. H. Smith Publishers, Inc.,
112 Madison Avenue, New York 10016

Published in England by Dragon's World Ltd,
Limpsfield and London

Gallery Books are available for bulk purchase for sales
promotions and premium use. For details write or telephone the
Manager of Special Sales, W. H. Smith Publishers, Inc.,
112 Madison Avenue, New York, New York 10016.
(212) 532-6600.

Editor: Michael Downey
Designer: Ann Doolan
Editorial Director: Pippa Rubinstein

Typeset by Bookworm Typesetting, Manchester, England
Printed in Singapore

Contents

Introduction

Many of the world's 3000-odd minerals are beautiful, even spectacular, and a visit to the mineral galleries of the major museums will show how wide is the range of colour and shape. Few collectors will be able to obtain large hand specimens of museum quality but many minerals can be found on mine dumps or can be purchased or traded.

After introducing the main rock types this guide concentrates upon the places which have produced, or are still producing, some of the best known minerals. Details of many of the major current and historical European localities are given for the first time in English.

The chemistry and crystallography of minerals have been treated in as much detail as necessary but no more. It is impossible not to give some of the reasons why minerals look the way they do and are found in some places and not others. Such information cannot be entirely expressed in simple terms.

Gemstones, which are rare, beautiful and durable varieties of minerals, are tested not only to establish their identity when fashioned but also to distinguish them from man-made materials. Details of these testing methods can be found in gemmological textbooks and are not described in detail here. Similarly the details of extraction methods for economic minerals are not given.

A glossary and a brief bibliography will help the reader to further his or her studies. May I strongly recommend anyone who decides to follow the rewarding study of rocks and minerals to find a good library which holds the major journals and geological maps? Go into the field only when you know where to go and what to look for.

Michael O'Donoghue

Proustite (East Germany)

Rocks

We can define a rock as a large mineral body which may contain only one mineral or several. Rocks often extend over considerable distances and form part of the earth's crust. Petrologists, who study rocks, recognize three rock classes and within each class a large number of different types are now known to be distinct; however many of the differences are of little concern to the general field worker and for that reason will not be discussed here.

Igneous rocks are formed from the molten state and are sometimes known as plutonic – the names are rather loosely used. The rocks are formed either from fast cooling intrusive lavas or from extrusive lava which has reached the surface by means of the well-known volcanic eruption. Plutonic rocks are formed at much greater depth and thus cool far more slowly.

Among the igneous rocks which are recognizable in the field is the natural glass obsidian. This forms an amorphous material since cooling is too quick for the constituent atoms to take up regular structural positions. Felsites are light coloured rocks with a fine-grained texture. Basalt arises from a lava solidified into a black rock, containing no quartz but rich in the feldspar minerals pyroxene and olivine. Old basalts with a coarse structure and found in sheets are often known as traprocks and are the home of many interesting minerals.

These are the extrusive igneous rocks. The intrusive rocks do not reach the surface but on rapid cooling may cut other rocks as seams (known as dikes). When the intrusive rock forms masses parallel to the structure of the rocks above them they are known as sheets or sills. In general crystals in these rocks are larger than those in extrusive rocks due to the greater time they have to grow before rapid cooling. Some intrusive rocks contain large crystals, often of the feldspar group and are known as porphyries. The individual crystals are called phenocrysts; other minerals that sometimes occur in this way are quartz, pyroxene and olivine. A common type of traprock is diabase in which lath-like crystals of feldspar grow first and darker minerals grow round them.

Among the plutonic rocks is the familiar granite with its coarse grain structure. It contains mostly quartz and orthoclase feldspar with some smaller amounts of a darker mineral. Pegmatites are very coarse-grained. Granites are usually light coloured and the mineral grains can be seen with the naked eye in many cases. Syenite is similar to granite but with no quartz.

Sandstone (South Dakota, USA)

A darker rock than granite but with a similar structure is diorite. These rocks are poor in quartz but rich in plagioclase feldspar. Darker and even poorer in silica than diorite is gabbro, containing a calcium-rich plagioclase and pyroxene as the dark mineral. Peridotite is a dark rock containing olivine or pyroxene with olivine. Pure olivine rock is known as dunite and pure pyroxene rock is pyroxenite. The serpentinized olivine in which diamonds are found is a peridotite, locally known as kimberlite.

As rock of whatever kind passes through its life on earth it is subjected to the action of ice, water and wind which gradually reduce it to its constituent particles. These find their way to the beds of rivers and streams or to estuaries, often along with their constituent minerals which are recovered alluvially. These particles or sediments on accumulation come to form sedimentary rocks as their grains are cemented by the heat and pressure generated by the accumulation process. These rocks form thick beds.

There are a number of sedimentary rock types. The rounded quartz pebbles cemented by finer material form a conglomerate and a similar type of rock is breccia with more angular particles. Sandstone is a very common type of sedimentary rock; arkose is formed by the mechanical disintegration of a granite. Shale is mostly made up of clay particles with some intermingled sand. Limestones are made up of calcium carbonate in a fine granular texture and are formed from lime removed from sea water by living marine organisms. Fossils display the types of creature living at the time of the original deposition. Dolomite resembles limestone but contains magnesium. Salt, coal and oil are associated with sedimentary deposits.

When a rock is altered by different types of geological event, involving heat and pressure either locally or extending over a large area, it is said to be metamorphosed. There will be alteration of the existing minerals and formation of new species. The commoner metamorphic rocks include slate, which represents a stage on the alteration of clay to mica and which shows a distinct cleavage following the mica plate direction. The original shale is sometimes cut at right angles by slate. Phyllite contains larger mica crystals than slate and may show a wavy rather than a flat surface.

Slate and phyllite are altered by pressure; the rock known as schist is formed by pressure and heat acting upon a mixture of hydrated and oxidized minerals. Shales with this composition alter to a rock largely made up of mica and mica schists are the home of a number of interesting minerals. Garnet, staurolite and andalusite are typical minerals of mica schists which may also provide beryl. The mica forms distinct bands which help to identify the rock.

Gneiss is similar but contains less mica – it may have been formed from a sandy shale or a sandstone with shale-like composition. Quartzite is a metamorphosed sandstone and forms a hard rock. Marble forms from the metamorphosis of limestone and may contain fossils from the original rock. When heat and pressure are accompanied by gases preceding an intrusion the existing sedimentary rock may alter and its minerals change. A number of silicate minerals such as garnet and epidote and some sulphides giving metallic ores arise from contact metamorphism.

Fine crystals of vesuvianite, garnet, scapolite and spinel can be found in altered limestones from places like Monte Somma. Lava on its journey to the surface saturates limestone with volcanic solutions and gases, thus forming a wide variety of minerals which are found in cavities in the rock on its reaching the surface.

Igneous Rocks

Granite

Nepheline syenite

Syenite

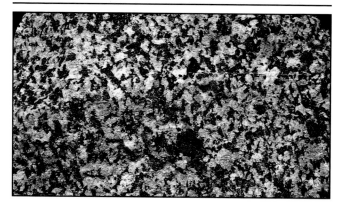

Diorite

Gabbro

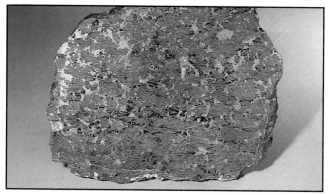

Peridotite

Dunite

Serpentinite

Rhyolite

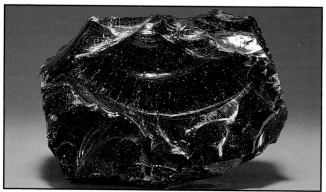

Obsidian

Trachyte

Andesite

Basalt

Metamorphic Rocks

Slate

Schist

Phyllite

Gneiss

Hornfels

Quartzite

Marble

Skarn

Sedimentary Rocks

Sandstone

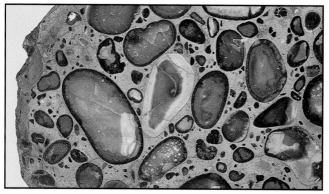

Conglomerate (pudding stone)

Limestone (fossiliferous)

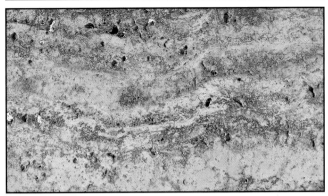

Travertine

Tufa

Flint

Chert

Shale

Minerals

Minerals are naturally-occurring inorganic substances with a definite and predictable chemical composition and physical properties. With the development of sophisticated testing methods it has become clear that many minerals fall into groups, the members of which have properties in common with each other; examples include the garnets, micas and zeolites. Rocks are made up of minerals (sometimes only one species) though not all minerals are rock-forming, and occupy great areas of the earth's crust. Minerals can quite often be identified by their appearance (colour and shape), whereas rocks usually need to be sliced into thin sections and examined under the microscope for their constituents to be established.

Though it is traditional to regard mineralogy as a study naturally linked with geology many workers today regard the discipline as a branch of chemistry dealing with natural substances. It is true that the appearance of minerals depends in the last resort on their chemical composition as does their crystal structure, and chemical relationships do illustrate the way in which particular species were formed. Petrologists have an affinity with mineralogists and with geologists since all three disciplines combine to identify economic mineral deposits.

Early mineralogists were men who first noticed workable metals or bright stones with ornamental potential. The way in which metal ores could be worked to provide the metal was discovered very early – before the recording of history – and in many ways methods have not changed very much though processing is now quicker and more effective. Though minerals were described by classical writers, the Middle Ages saw a decline into magical and fanciful corruptions of earlier efforts to give objective accounts of objects actually seen. It was not until Georg Bauer (1494-1555), whose Latin name was Georgius Agricola, began work on his *De re metallica* and other books that a serious attempt to describe and group minerals could be seen to be in progress. His *De natura fossilium* has been regarded as the first mineralogical textbook as it contains an elementary classification of minerals according to established and tested properties. This type of classification is usually called taxonomy in other sciences; 'descriptive mineralogy' is preferred as a phrase in earth science circles. The first worker to make a serious attempt to standardize terms and descriptions based on the appearance of a specimen was Abraham Gottlob Werner (1750-1817), a German geologist.

Gypsum (Chihuahua, Mexico)

As mineralogists studied more and more specimens it became clear that many showed characteristic external shapes, directions in which they broke easily, variation of colour with direction, and differing abilities to resist abrasion. Thus the study of crystallography began. Until the development of x-ray testing, however, scientists were unable to determine the exact nature of crystal structures. Steno (the Dane Niels Stensen, 1638-1686) was the first to discover that, on crystals, the angle between like pairs of faces on different examples of the same species was always the same; he made a series of measurements on quartz crystals from different places. This constancy of interfacial angles helped to establish knowledge of crystal structure and of how crystals were formed. Such laws also finally routed the ideas of magical formation. The development of a simple instrument to measure interfacial angles paved the way for the study of many species and the establishment of descriptions of crystal morphology or shape. The amassing of many observations allowed laws to be drawn up to which crystal symmetry could be referred. The further study of these laws eventually proved the nature of the building blocks from which a crystal is built up.

With the discovery of x-rays by Röntgen in 1895 and the discovery of the way in which they could pass through solid bodies and be reflected by planes of atoms (by Max von Laue in 1912) the internal structure of crystals could at last be visualized and recorded. Later work was able to show exactly where the atoms were in a crystal. Once this was known the cause of crystalline properties could also be deduced.

Mineral Classification

Minerals arranged in a mineral gallery of a major museum follow chemical classification and all descriptive mineralogy books follow the same treatment. Usually, chemical classification groups together minerals with the same simple or complex anion. If you need to compare the various minerals of an element which always forms cations (copper or sodium are examples) you need to look through all the anionic groups or in the index. The major mineral groups below are discussed in order of their abundance in the earth's crust.

Silicates

Silicon is next to oxygen in abundance in the earth's crust. It forms the tetrahedrally coordinated complex silicate anion with oxygen, $(SiO_4)^{4-}$. Silicates are the most abundant minerals in the crust and since the SiO_4 tetrahedra can join in several ways the variety of silicate minerals is considerable. The tetrahedra occur as separate unlinked units or as chains, sheets, rings, double chains, frameworks or pairs. Water is often present and in the zeolite group it can escape when the minerals are mined since it is so loosely bound. Hydroxyl (OH) is found in many silicates but is an essential part of the structure and cannot be easily removed. In silicates with independent tetrahedra the SiO_4 groups are held together by interspersed cations. The olivine and garnet groups are examples. Crystals are dense and hard and show an equidimensional form. Silicates with pairs of tetrahedra are rare but ring silicates are more commonly found. The symmetry depends on the number of SiO_4 groups in the ring. Beryl is a major example; rings give elongated crystals of moderate density and considerable hardness. Chain and double-chain silicates, closely related, form the major mineral groups pyroxene and amphibole respectively. Diopside and jadeite are members of the pyroxene group; asbestos reflects the often fibrous form of the amphiboles.

In sheet silicates the tetrahedra are linked into separate sheets or layers held together by cations. This group includes the micas, clays, and talc. Minerals of this group are easily split into thin wafers. Framework silicates include quartz and the feldspar group. Rigid, partially covalent bonding in framework silicates gives them fairly loose structures and the minerals are hard but not very dense.

Oxides

Oxide minerals have oxygen as the sole anion. When the sole anion is the complex anion (OH) minerals are hydroxides.

Many oxides are hard and compact, as corundum; this is the case when the cations are much smaller than the O^{2-} anion. Spinel, cassiterite, and chromite are important oxides.

Phosphates
Phosphates have the complex anion $(PO_4)^{3-}$. As in silicates PO_4 tetrahedra can occur separately in crystal structures or can form pairs or rings. Apatite is the commonest phosphate mineral.

Carbonates
Carbonates contain the complex anion $(CO_3)^{2-}$ and are an important mineral group. Many carbonates are of organic origin; the most prominent example is $CaCO_3$, calcite. The triangular CO_3 group gives threefold symmetry to the carbonates; where the cation is comparatively large the ions pack to give orthorhombic symmetry (as in witherite, $BaCO_3$). Most carbonates are soft and soluble in dilute acids.

Sulphates
Sulphur is found as the pure element, as the anion S^{2-} in sulphides and as the complex anion $(SO_4)^{2-}$ in sulphates. Most sulphates occur in sedimentary rocks and are often associated with salt deposits because they are precipitated from evaporating bodies of highly saline water in landlocked lakes or at the margins of seas in hot desert areas.

Sulphides
Sulphides have the anion S^{2-} and crystallize where the oxygen concentration is so low that sulphates cannot be formed. Many of the chief metal ores are sulphides. The density is usually high and the variable hardness usually low. Metal and sulphur atoms link in a variety of structures, more commonly bonded covalently than ionically. Pyrite is usually the first sulphide to be encountered.

Halides
Halides have as their anion one of the group of elements known as halogens; fluorine, chlorine, bromine and iodine. The bonding is usually ionic and many minerals are cubic. Fluorite is a common example.

Aragonite (Utah, USA)

Crystals

Crystal Morphology

The term morphology means the general shape of a crystal. In field identification work it is vital to be able to predict the type of symmetry shown by a crystal from a fragment which may show only a few features. Details of how crystals grow can be found in all books on crystals and in large mineralogical textbooks. For identification we need to know how a crystal gets its overall recognizable shape, or form.

The external shape of a crystal is determined by its atomic structure and the smooth faces are directly related to the way in which atoms are deposited in particular directions, and to the size of the atoms. The atomic structure is also responsible for crystallographic properties like cleavage, directional hardness and pleochroism. The angles between adjacent faces in a particular species are always the same for that species and this is one of the first features to look for in the field. A simple instrument, the goniometer, can be improvised very easily and can quickly measure important angles even when the specimen is quite small. The angles can also be measured on an optical goniometer but this has to be done in the laboratory.

Mathematically there are 230 space groups possible in nature – that is 230 different three-dimensional lattices all of which could in theory have an actual crystal representative. In practice there is no representative for some of the space groups. The 230 space groups can be divided into 32 classes and these in turn into seven crystal systems, each of which can be described in general terms by referring them to a set of *crystallographic axes* or *axes of reference*. The concept of axes is important for the study of crystals; if we take a cube we see that there can be straight lines drawn through the crystal from the centre of the faces, from corner to corner and so on. Turning the crystal through quarter, half, and three-quarter turns repeats the same shape you began with, or appears to. When this happens the axis about which the crystal is turned is an *axis of symmetry*. It is easy to follow these on a cube, harder on less symmetrical crystals which are in the majority! Crystals may also have *planes of symmetry* – directions in which a crystal could be split into two portions, each the mirror image of the other. Crystals may also have a *centre of symmetry*, a point within the crystal which has similar faces and edges on each side. A cube shows the highest degree of crystalline symmetry and has more planes and axes of symmetry than any other crystal form. Other crystals

Wulfenite (Arizona, USA)

may show lesser symmetry on a scale at the bottom of which come crystals with very low symmetry. Looking back at the cube we can refer it to three crystallographic axes of equal length and meeting at right angles. There are 9 planes and 13 axes of symmetry in a cube with faces identical with each other – striations (parallel grooves) on some cube faces and not on others lowers their symmetry.

The cube can be modified to an octahedron by cutting off each corner – the octahedron belongs to the same crystal system as the cube. If a low 4-faced pyramid was built on each face we would then have a 24-faced form, the icositetrahedron (different texts frequently give different names to the forms of the cubic system). In the field *cubic system* crystals will appear at least spherical even if clear faces cannot be distinguished.

Cubic system

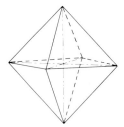

Octahedron

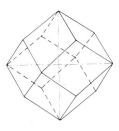

Rhombic dodecahedron

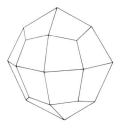

Icositetrahedron

In descending order of symmetry comes the *tetragonal system*. Its crystallographic axes number three; they intersect at right angles and two are equal in length with the third either longer or shorter. Crystals usually show a square cross-section and well-developed prismatic form (faces meeting in parallel edges)

Tetragonal system

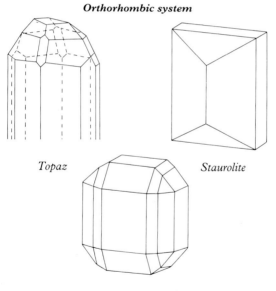

Prismatic crystals of zircon

Vesuvianite

Orthorhombic system

Topaz

Staurolite

Olivine

with a pyramidal termination. Some minerals crystallize as tetragonal bipyramids which resemble the octahedra of the cubic system. In the tetragonal system the prism may be first or second order depending on whether the face cuts one horizontal axis and is parallel to the other or whether each face cuts both axes at an equal distance from the centre. The form known as the pinacoid – usually in pairs – cuts the vertical axis and is parallel to both the horizontal ones. The pyramid forms may be first or second order.

The *orthorhombic system* is referred to three axes which intersect at right angles but which are unequal to one another. Crystals are usually placed with the longest axis (the c-axis) vertical and the shortest axis (the a-axis) towards the observer. The axis running from left to right is styled the b-axis. Forms include the prism, pyramid and pinacoid; pyramid forms cut all the crystallographic axes, produced where necessary.

Monoclinic system

Epidote

Orthoclase

The *monoclinic system* has three crystallographic axes, none equal in length and one being at right angles to the other two which are not at right angles to each other. Conventionally the crystals are described with the tilted (clino)axis facing the observer. Prisms, domes (forms intersecting the vertical and one other axis but parallel to the third, also found in the orthorhombic system) and pyramids are found.

The *triclinic system* has three unequal axes meeting at angles which are not right angles. This gives symmetry only with pairs of faces which can be placed bottom and top or front and back. Usually the pinacoid form is the only one needing description.

Crystals of the *hexagonal system* are referred to a vertical axis at right angles to three axes intersecting each other at 60°. These three are equal in length, the vertical axis being longer or shorter. Forms are the hexagonal prism with development of first and second order prisms as in the tetragonal system. Crystals are often terminated by the pyramid form, which can also be first or second order, depending upon whether two or three of the horizontal axes are cut.

Similar to the hexagonal system but with a three-fold rather

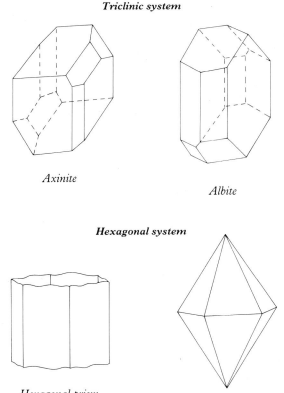

Triclinic system

Axinite

Albite

Hexagonal system

Hexagonal prism

Hexagonal bipyramid

than a six-fold symmetry is the *trigonal system*. Crystals often show a triangular cross-section as in tourmaline and the rhombohedral class has axes paralleling the rhombohedron edges. The rhombohedron is developed by the dominant growth of every other face, this pattern of growth alternating from top to bottom of the crystal. A rhombohedron has six faces and if the angles were 90° would be the same as a cube standing on a corner with the vertical axis protruding from the point. Usually with the rhombohedral class the horizontal axes are oriented as coming out of the equatorial edges.

We can now see that crystals can be quite precisely classified even though we have only discussed the ideal cases in each system. We know that the outward appearance of a crystal is dictated by its underlying atomic structure – the term 'form',

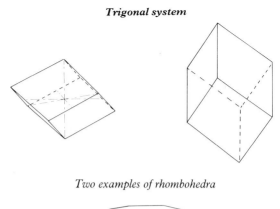

Two examples of rhombohedra

Tabular crystal of corundum

though often loosely used for 'general shape', should really be used to denote faces inclining in the same way to the crystal axes and reflecting exactly the same underlying atomic pattern. Form is, in fact, the assemblage of possible faces in a crystal when the planes, axes and centres of symmetry act together. It can be deduced from an imperfect specimen by the presence or absence of right angles, surface markings and similar face dimensions. Many crystals are said to have *open form*, that is, they need more than one form to be present to enclose space. Prismatic crystals (with faces meeting in parallel edges) need the pyramid, pinacoid or dome to complete them; crystals consisting entirely of a single form (octahedron, rhombic dodecahedron, for example) are *closed forms*. Many crystals show a combination of forms in such a way that it is clear that growth oscillated between two possible forms; this is usually detected by the presence of fine lines bevelling adjacent faces. All forms in the cubic (isometric) system are closed; all forms in the monoclinic and triclinic systems are open.

Crystalline Properties

When a crystal breaks it may fracture randomly with a more or less well-developed shell-like conchoidal fracture. When a crystal breaks along a *crystallographic direction* significant for its species it is said to *cleave*. The term 'perfect' is used for

Twinned crystals

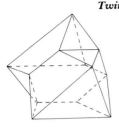

Diamond

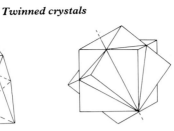

Fluorite

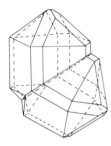

Cassiterite

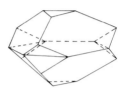

Calcite

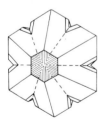

Chrysoberyl

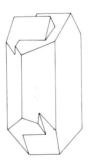

Orthoclase

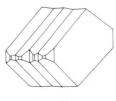

Albite

cleavage surfaces of exceptional smoothness as in diamond or mica; good, fair, poor, and indistinct are self-explanatory. It should be remembered that if a cleavage develops along a particular atomic plane it will also develop along other planes like it in the same crystal structure. In the cubic system diamond and fluorite show octahedral cleavage (four directions) and sphalerite six directions. The tetragonal system often shows good prismatic or basal pinacoidal cleavage as in apophyllite. Perfect rhombohedral cleavage is found in the trigonal system; it is generally less prominent in the hexagonal system. The monoclinic system and the orthorhombic systems show basal pinacoidal cleavage as in topaz and the pyroxene and amphibole groups. It should be remembered that there are some deceptive minerals which pretend to have a cleavage characteristic of another mineral, as when the prismatic pyroxene cleavage is mistaken for square prismatic tetragonal cleavage.

Parting is another form of breaking along planes of weakness, especially in twinned crystals (see below). It is particularly common in the corundum minerals. Partings develop in limited numbers in any crystal whereas cleavages can occur in unlimited numbers in any crystal. Generally parting directions are quite widely separated from one another while cleavages are very close.

Some crystals grow together in special ways known as *twinning*. Twinned crystals are identified most easily by the presence of re-entrant angles which look like V-shaped notches in the edges. The individual twins meet along the composition plane. In the absence or obscurity of re-entrant angles look for changes of lustre in parallel bands (as in sphalerite) or for lamellae (polysynthetic twinning) where individual crystals are placed together like sheets on paper in a book (lamellae) – each page is reversed with respect to its neighbours.

Interpenetrant twins – the term is self explanatory – are characteristic of many minerals, particularly of fluorite. When crystals twin on several sides at once they are known as cyclic twins; the pseudo-hexagonal twinning of chrysoberyl is very notable and attractive. Twinning in quartz is virtually universal; Dauphiné, Brazil and Japan twins are the most common types and twinning in this mineral is an excellent guide to identification.

Identifying Minerals

Hardness

To the mineralogist the hardness of a specimen is its ability to resist abrasion or scratching. The scale of hardness still in use today was devised by Friedrich Mohs (1773-1839). It is not a linear scale and is not diagnostic, save in the case of diamond (at the top of the scale), but it does give an idea of the strength of a particular mineral as even the small groove made on a specimen involves the separation of atoms.

Mohs' scale

10 Diamond
 9 Corundum
 8 Topaz
 7 Quartz
 6 Feldspar
 5 Apatite
 4 Fluorite
 3 Calcite
 2 Gypsum
 1 Talc

All that the scale tells us is that mineral no. 4 scratches mineral no. 3 and those below. In practice many minerals lie between the whole numbers and may be shown as 6.5 and so on. Other tests, often based on indentation, are also used but these are not field tests and for that reason are not further discussed.

The actual application of hardness tests is simple though there are dangers. A set of hardness pencils is the only tool needed. These are pencils with the graphite points replaced by sharp-edged pieces of the standard scale minerals. The wood of the 'pencil' is replaced by metal. The area to be tested should be the pure mineral, not a coating and without grain or cracks. If such a surface is not immediately apparent, remove a small section if possible. The pencil should be drawn across the test surface with a firm but not heavy pressure (too hard a pressure may start cleavages). Change the direction if the point slides rather than bites. Always observe the test through a lens or microscope and wipe off the powder. With experience the tester can feel the scratch and there is no need to make a long indentation. Start with corundum and go down the scale.

If no hardness testing set is available remember that the fingernail has a hardness of about 2.5 and the blade of a

penknife about 5-5.5. A filed needle in a holder can also be most useful. Oxides and silicates are usually hard, halides, carbonates and sulphates are usually soft and may show an easy cleavage. Native metals are sectile (they can be peeled) and malleable (they can be beaten out into thin sheets).

Mineral names follow certain conventions. The suffix -ide usually denotes a compound with two components, such as sodium chloride, silver sulphide. When two valence states exist for the positive elements (written first in the formula) a suffix will sometimes indicate which state is present. The most common example is iron, which in its divalent state is said to be ferrous as in ferrous oxide (FeO), or in its trivalent state as ferric (Fe_2O_3). Prefixes can be used to indicate the number of atoms in negative elements (shown on the right-hand side of the formula). Examples are titanium dioxide for rutile (TiO_2), arsenic trisulphide for orpiment (As_2S_3).

Growth of Crystals

Mineral crystals grow from solutions in which ions which will form the solid are dissolved, from molten solids or from vapours carrying the needed ions mixed up with those of the gas. Solution-grown crystals often show the best forms with molten solid growth coming next. Crystals grown from the vapour phase may also show fine quality though there are fewer examples. A good example of crystal growth from the melt can be seen in granite which shows grey quartz crystals, pink feldspar and black mica.

As a molten rock cools, structures made up of ions begin to take shape and build the symmetrical lattices shown by all crystals. When the melt is exhausted no more growth takes place. Minerals which crystallized first are more likely to show faces recognizable as crystal faces, even though they have formed in solid rock. Later crystallized minerals are more likely to be found as grains. Diamond, corundum and garnet crystals have often managed to get their faces formed before interference from other minerals took place as cooling progressed.

Crystals found in rock cavities have usually grown from water solutions. Substances which will not dissolve in water at normal temperatures and pressure may dissolve when temperature and pressure is raised. When an ore vein is prospected a sequence of minerals may be observed from top to bottom, the minerals being distinguished from one another by reason of the temperature and pressure conditions appropriate for growth. Quartz, calcite, zeolites and clay minerals grow

Vanadinite (Morocco)

from solutions; laboratory growth of quartz is known as hydrothermal growth and this parallels the way in which quartz grows in nature, in which the term hydrothermal is also used.

Crystals grown from the vapour are usually found in the vicinity of fumaroles in volcanic areas. Vaporized minerals are dissolved in gases and deposit on cooler surfaces. Sulphur crystals are by far the finest grown by this process.

A crystal can only grow when it has a nucleus of a critical size around which to grow. If no such nucleus (a grain of dust might be sufficient) is available then groups of atoms come together just long enough to form a suitable nucleus. Accidental formation of a nucleus is more likely when temperature is reduced. Fastest crystal growth occurs when the arrival of fresh material on the surface makes sites available for further deposition. This type of growth gives rise to screw dislocations and results in a growth spiral on the face of the crystal. Dislocations are common in crystals and this particular variety eventually forms a flat hump on the face. Screw dislocations help crystals to grow since fresh nuclei do not have to be continually produced. Dislocation-free crystals (usually made in the laboratory) grow as minute parts of a fresh layer built up by chance on a crystal face; as the new layer is only partially covering the face it forms a step whose edge itself provides a site for fresh particles to be deposited. This partial layer expands to cover the entire face and a new partial layer has to arise by chance before growth can continue.

When new layers of atoms are deposited rapidly on a particular face the crystal grows fast at right angles to this face. The face gets smaller as fresh material is deposited. The best developed faces of the final crystals are those which have built up at the slowest rate. Preferential growth of edges and corners reflects fluctuation in the supply of feed material – this type of growth is seen at its most extreme in hopper crystals or the growth of dendrites (plant-like crystals). Inclusions which greatly help in the identification of transparent crystals also arise through circumstances of crystal growth. Details can be found in textbooks of gemstone identification.

It is also interesting to note that some faces of a crystal appear smooth and others rough. The larger the face the more likely it is to become damaged through accidents of growth since it takes longer to grow. A crystal with noticeably perfect faces may be artificial, particularly if it is large and clear. Much quartz is laboratory grown and crystals may reach very large sizes. Some crystals may grow over another of a different species as in quartz on calcite and rutile on hematite. Some faces attract overgrowth more than others and this can be seen in the colouring of alternate faces of quartz by red hematite.

Old overgrowths may themselves be overgrown and this gives rise, again prominently in quartz, to phantom crystals. Sceptre quartz arises where the tips of growing crystals have readier access to feed material than crystal sections closer to the walls of the cavity in which they are growing. Etch marks (pits) on the faces of some crystals are a useful indication of the mineral's symmetry and result from changes in the growth conditions which cause the crystal to dissolve rather than grow further.

The general shape of a crystal is called its habit and is intimately linked with crystal form, itself dictated by the operation of the symmetry elements of planes, axes and centres of symmetry. Some minerals have so characteristic a habit that they can be identified by it alone. Habits of single crystals include: *acicular*, needle-like as in natrolite; *capillary*, hair-like as in millerite; *columnar*, as in beryl or tourmaline; *platy*, the micas; *bladed*, as in kyanite; *tabular*, flat as in some corundum and wulfenite; *dendritic*, tree- or branch-like as in native copper and silver; *wedge-shaped*, as in gypsum; *spear-shaped*, as in descloizite.

Many minerals do not occur as recognizable single crystals but as masses with no characteristic external form. They may be one of several mineral species. Radiating or fan-like shapes will help to identify them and some of these aggregates can be described.

Botryoidal: like a bunch of grapes as in malachite
Reniform: kidney-shaped as in hematite
Mammillary: breast-shaped as in spherulitic or globular masses
Fibrous: as in the asbestos minerals
Stalactitic: resembling hanging stalactites
Foliated or lamellar: easily split leaves or sheets
Plumose: plume-like
Divergent or radiated: spreading like a fan from a single point
Stellate: forming a star
Reticulated: thin crystals in a net-like formation
Dendritic: plant-like
Arborescent: tree-like

The characteristic appearance of the mineral surface as seen by reflected light is known as its *lustre* and this property can be roughly classified as adamantine (the lustre of diamond), vitreous (glassy – most minerals), metallic, submetallic, resinous or oily, pearly or silky (cleavage surfaces and fibrous minerals), earthy or dull.

Some crystals have electrical properties which may help in identification. Tourmaline is pyroelectric in that it becomes electrically charged when heated. In this way dust is attracted.

Quartz crystals show piezoelectricity – they develop small electric voltages when under pressure. This is a most useful property and is the basis of many electronic instruments.

Crystals and Light

Crystals reflect light to give a particular lustre and refract it when they are transparent. Refraction is a slowing-down of the velocity of the incident light as it passes through the crystal. If the incident light is broken into two rays on entering the crystal each ray travels at a different velocity and the crystal is said to be anisotropic or doubly refractive. In isotropic crystals (or amorphous substances) the incident ray is not split into two.

The important property of the refractive index is a simple relationship between the sine of the angle of incidence and the sine of the angle of refraction – the sines bear a constant ratio to each other for the two media in contact and for light of the same colour. Minerals of the orthorhombic, monoclinic and triclinic systems will have three refractive indices, all variable, two in one plane and the third at right angles to this plane so that only two readings can be taken at one time. Minerals in the tetragonal, hexagonal, and trigonal systems have two refractive indices, one of which is unvarying. These minerals have one direction in which the incident ray traverses the crystal unrefracted; this is known as an optic axis. Minerals with one optic axis are said to be uniaxial. Minerals with three refractive indices have two optic axes and are said to be biaxial.

When readings are taken (this is usually most easily seen in comparatively large transparent crystals such as those of gem quality minerals) uniaxial minerals will have the fixed index (the ordinary ray) at a higher or lower reading than the moveable (extraordinary) ray. Where the extraordinary has the higher reading the mineral is said to be optically positive. In biaxial minerals the highest reading is called gamma, the lowest alpha; beta is an intermediate index. Where alpha and beta are closer together than gamma and beta the mineral is optically positive. In all optical tests the position of the optic axis should be remembered as inaccurate readings can result if it is forgotten. In uniaxial minerals the optic axis is always parallel to the vertical crystal axis. In biaxial specimens the optic axes do not take up predictable positions.

Ordinary light consists of components which vibrate in all directions at right angles to the direction of travel. This is known as unpolarized light. When a ray is refracted into two rays, each is plane polarized with respect to the other – that is, the vibration takes place in only one direction parallel to the

Sulphur (Sicily)

direction of travel. A number of important tests make use of this property. Two pieces of the plastic material Polaroid placed so that each cuts off vibrations in a direction at right angles to that of the other will indicate to the observer whether a transparent mineral placed between them in this 'crossed' position is isotropic or anisotropic.

Fifteen different causes of colour have been identified for natural and man-made substances. Many minerals owe their colour to elements either part of their normal chemical composition or occurring as partial substitutes for those elements. The transition elements (numbers 22-29 of the periodic table) play an important part in the colouration of gem minerals although they do not colour anything like all of them. Some examples include: titanium acting with iron to give a blue colour to many minerals, including blue sapphire (a variety of corundum); vanadium is thought to give colour in some blue minerals and green in some emeralds and other beryls; chromium gives the red of ruby and red spinel and the green of emerald and jadeite; iron gives red, green, yellow or blue, in rather subdued shades – examples include yellow sapphire, peridot and blue spinel; cobalt gives pink in most natural minerals and blue in man-made blue glasses and spinels; nickel gives a bright apple-green as in chrysoprase; copper gives a blue or green as in turquoise and malachite.

Colour may be altered by heating or irradiation, natural or artificial. Play of colour as opposed to body colour as discussed above can arise from dispersion (diamond is the best-known example); this occurs when white light is broken into its component spectrum colours each of which is refracted by a different amount, the red least and the violet most. The greater the difference in refractive index the higher the dispersion.

Colours produced by interference are quieter than dispersion colours and can be seen on soap bubbles and oil slicks. White light falling on to a thin film (cracks or cleavage surfaces) produces a series of spectrum colours as some components of the incident beam are retarded by passing through to the lower side of the film, rejoining the main beam either in or out of phase. Anisotropic minerals show pleochroism, a change of colour with direction. Generally two shades of the same colour are seen but, in some cases, two or three colours (the specimen needs to be turned to see all of them) may be a useful clue to identity. Minerals like cordierite, alexandrite, and chrysoberyl show three distinct colours; corundum and beryl show two. Long- and short-wave ultraviolet radiation (LWUV and SWUV) is a useful test for some minerals. They will glow various colours and some will phosphoresce, continuing to glow after the radiation is turned off.

Conservation and Collecting

The places where fine crystals can be found are very few, since
several conditions for growth have to be present at the same
time. Naturally collectors gravitate to these places and a party
can do a great deal of damage, especially if hammers are used
(in general they are not often vital since plenty of dump
material is good enough for laboratory investigation). It should
also be remembered that mineral deposits are owned by
someone – there is no land without an owner – and farmland
can often be seriously affected by the careless leaving open of
gates and the dropping of rubbish which may harm animals. If
the site is a quarry careful arrangements with respect to
equipment, places to look and timing must be made well in
advance. In the United States and Canada many incidents are
on record involving amateurs who have damaged expensive
machinery and by their actions have closed sites to others.
There is a certain 'macho' element among amateur collectors –
not unknown in the United Kingdom – which somehow
equates scientific achievement with the number of underground
visits undertaken. Do not fall for this attitude which has a
superficial charm when a group is sitting over its beer: to go
underground in a non-working mine is sheer folly unless you
are accompanied by someone (preferably several people) who
really knows the mine.

Before venturing into the field serious collectors or students
should get hold of geological and mining maps and records of
visits made by others. Few things separate the amateur collector
from the serious student so much as their approach to this
aspect of field work. There are not many collections of
geological material and many of the existing ones are not
readily accessible to amateurs since they are in the major
university libraries which restrict access to their members.
Similarly the average collector will have no access to the library
of the Geological Society of London since it is restricted to
Fellows of the Society. Nonetheless, access to records is vital
and somehow those with a genuine will to find out more about
minerals, whether or not they are collected, will find a way to
get at what they need. It really is a matter of life or death when
you are in a mine – only a plan will show where water on the
floor covers a deep shaft and is more than a puddle. It is also
vital to know how mining has been carried out in the past. Long
blasting may have weakened the roof so that even a shout will
bring it down.

Details of equipment and clothing can be found in many
other mineral books but it is important to know what kind of

hammer to take into the field, even if it stays in your rucksack. Geological hammers have a square head on one side and a chisel edge on the other – this may be replaced by a pick. Weight varies from half a pound to around four pounds, according to the task you want it to do. Sledge hammers should not normally be needed. A steel chisel is also very useful for removing crystals – if these are very small and delicate use a dental tool or, better still, leave them where they are! The blade of a pocket knife is useful for hardness testing as well as for extracting crystals from the softer types of rock. The 10x lens is vital for the study of fine-grained rock and small crystals. 10x is the most useful magnification since higher magnifications involve critical focal lengths and make handling difficult.

Serious collectors can and should join a well-organized mineral or geological club where one exists. Standards of clubs vary a good deal, many working through the same programme and speakers year after year and nobody seeming to learn anything new. On the other hand well-run clubs extend the knowledge and ambitions of their members and really try to get good outside speakers from the professional earth science world.

Remarks made above about geological literature apply equally to geological maps. Try to get in touch with the Geological Survey of your country or with the Survey of the place you are intending to visit. The British Geological Survey publishes the eighteen guides of *British Regional Geology* which cover the whole of the country. Maps will show major geological features, especially if the scale is large; pegmatites and mineralized veins can be shown together with areas of contact metamorphism. Note that even the British Isles are not completely covered by published geological maps even today and similar conditions obtain in other countries.

Collecting Hints

Many well-formed crystals are found projecting into cavities and it is usually easier and safer to try to get part of the matrix to which the crystals are attached. This will save undue handling of perhaps delicate crystals. Generally it is better to display crystals on their matrix as it shows them off better and adds strength to the whole specimen. When matrix (which is rock) has to be removed try to find out how it will break. Rocks usually split or break in particular directions – schists and bedded rocks are good examples so it is a good idea to make use of these directions.

When collecting from pegmatites note that the cleavage

Apophyllite (Canada)

directions of the fragments are usually bounded by the cleavage directions of the very large crystal constituents. Calcite, which is often found as fine crystals, has an easy cleavage and will disintegrate into its constituent rhombs if too roughly extracted. Here a supporting matrix is vital.

The importance of keeping field notes is mentioned elsewhere but do make sure that each specimen is wrapped and labelled as soon as you find it. Transporting your finds is a matter for thought. Fine and delicate specimens should be carried flat with nothing on top of them. For ease of carrying large and heavy specimens of less fragility a back-pack is easier to manage than a shoulder bag. Choose a strong bag.

Cleaning Specimens

Mineral specimens come in all states and conditions and since many of the three thousand or so known species occur as dusts, crusts or powders most cannot be cleaned at all and have to be displayed as found. Many are unsuitable for display since they may be light – or heat – sensitive. Still others may be water-soluble, and opal, for example, may need to be kept in a liquid. Many undergo a stealthy chemical change which merely continues what had already begun in geological time and sometimes this alteration can affect their fellow minerals or the materials of the case in which they are kept.

Gem quality minerals – and there are relatively few of them – are generally able to stand up to hard knocks and abrasion by siliceous airborne dust. But even these may show perfect cleavage or be brittle (very many minerals are brittle) so that ultrasonic cleaners should not be used on them.

The care of a specimen begins just before you find it. If you are on a dump don't throw rocks around; they may fall on fine specimens and ruin them. They may also fall on your friends or even on you. If you are recovering specimens from a mine (few collectors can or should do this) watch the formation or condition of seams or pockets. Failure to do this followed by indiscriminate hammering can destroy what you have come for. Once out of the ground or free from the dump wrap the specimen and label the wrapper, at the same time noting the occurrence in your field book, with details of what else was there and of the formations from which the specimen was obtained. It is amazingly easy to forget where you have found something, even when you are back at base only a few hours afterwards.

Never wrap more than one specimen in the same wrapping – they will jostle in transport and break pieces off one another; cleavages may develop and you may finish up with more specimens than you began with. Remember most mineral locations are in rough country (from the point of view of a fragile mineral all country is rough) and you will be walking over it. Vehicular transport is also subject to bumps and you may not be able to tell at the end of the day what your specimens are, so badly may they break and intermingle.

Once back at home or museum, place your specimens somewhere safe and label them if they are not already labelled adequately. There are lots of ways in which this can be done. Link up field notes and final specimen label by means of accession numbers – and do it at once. Try not to so mark a specimen that the mark itself appears to have some mineralogical significance; a sticky label is usually better than an ink marking though peeling a label from a fragile specimen may damage the surface and Indian ink should do no harm to hard ore minerals.

Once in from the field the specimens will usually need to be cleaned (but establish which are which first). Remove soil with a soft brush, taking care not to knock off small crystals; use a harder brush or wooden probe where the soil is compacted. Do not use metal – it will damage soft minerals. If your material is in gravel form (with luck the gem gravels of Sri Lanka) sieve it into a sink, screen it, and ensure that the plug is in the sink! If you have collected large rock or mineral specimens with matrix (rock or other minerals adhering to them) do not try to remove the matrix with sharp blows with any tool – cleavages may start. In the same way clamping large specimens to work on them can itself damage them through the exertion of pressure in critical directions. Coatings such as mica can be removed with a stiff brush. Adhering minerals which have a cleavage themselves can be picked off in cleavage directions; calcite is a good example. Residues may need to be dissolved away with acids; dilute hydrochloric acid is probably the most useful though take care that the specimen itself is not soluble in whatever substance you choose!

If an ultrasonic cleaner is used on specimens which will not be adversely affected, use water with a little detergent as the cleaning liquid. In general minerals are not water-soluble but there are some important exceptions so try to identify your find first. Particularly likely to dissolve are some nitrates, borates and sulphates. Alcohol is probably the most useful cleaning agent for these minerals, should they need to be cleaned at all, but do not use it near a naked flame. Alcohol can be used for the quick drying of specimens that have been immersed in water. Acetone, with uses similar to those of alcohol, should also be kept away from flames.

Seriously disfiguring stains can be removed with acids but some of them are so dangerous that their use is best left to museums and universities. Amateurs should not use them. The most dangerous is hydrofluoric acid (HF). This needs to be kept in polyethylene containers as it will attack some metals and plastics. Never inhale it or let it touch the skin. If it does splash, use continuously running water to wash it off and get medical attention at once. Never pour HF from one container to another nor leave it unattended or unsecured. Used acid should be neutralized by adding calcite and washing away with water.

Dangerous though HF is, the cleaning of silicates which remain unaffected by its action is admittedly helped; it removes feldspar coatings from tourmaline and beryl though specimens should not be left long in the acid as faces may become etched. Coat portions of specimens that do not need to be treated with wax (beeswax will do) which can later be dissolved by acetone. Rinse with water for several hours at least after HF treatment. Remember that if you are using HF and look round to find you are in your own home you should not be there or be using the acid. If you use the acid outside do not stand to windward of it.

Also useful for the cleaning of silicates is ammonium bifluoride (NH_4HF_2) which is less dangerous than HF. But remember that it will form HF when mixed with warm water so care still needs to be taken. It is also slower to act than HF. Remember to protect surfaces which you don't want to clean.

Yet another dangerous but useful cleaning agent is sodium cyanide. This should not be inhaled or allowed to touch the skin – never work with ANY of these acids unless you know what you are doing and always use a fume cupboard. Sodium cyanide is used to clean gold, silver and copper. Concentrated nitric, sulphuric and hydrochloric acids are also dangerous but their use in concentrated form is not usually necessary for cleaning specimens. They are usually diluted for use – remember to add acid to water, not water to acid and pour the acid in a gentle but steady stream. Hydrochloric acid (HCl) is used to clean carbonates, dissolving the calcite coating with a solution of 5-10%. Keep in plastic or glass containers, never in metals ones. Watch for signs of acid eating through the walls of plastic containers!

Sulphuric acid H_2SO_4 should be kept in glass containers and is less often used for cleaning. Some hydrous minerals may lose their water when in contact with sulphuric acid whose use in such circumstances is not recommended. Nitric acid should be stored in glass and in the dark. The acid decomposes on exposure to light, releasing dangerous fumes of nitrogen dioxide. It is rarely used for cleaning. The liquid aqua regia, which will dissolve gold, is made of nitric acid with

Marcasite (Czechoslovakia)

hydrochloric acid in the proportion of one part to three. Platinum will dissolve in a mixture of two parts nitric to nine parts hydrochloric acids. Some calcite encrustations can be removed with acetic acid – again the concentrated form is dangerous and the fumes should never be inhaled. Oxalic acid is used to remove persistent brown iron stains which are usually the mineral limonite. Warm dilute hydrochloric acid is almost as good in this context and much safer.

If you find you have to use an acid for cleaning – be honest, is your specimen that important? – try it out on an inconspicuous part first. Material with lots of cracks will respond more quickly than unflawed pieces and watch to see the varying rates at which the cleaning agent works. Don't go away and let the reaction proceed on its own. HF will remove clay minerals from beryl before the beryl begins to be affected.

Many minerals are soluble in something and the following table is a guide.

These classes are usually water-soluble:

Nitrates
Hydroxides (some)
Chlorides (apart from lead, silver and mercuric chlorides)
Carbonates (only ammonium, potassium and sodium carbonates)
Borates containing water of crystallization
Sulphates (but not barium, calcium or lead sulphates)
Phosphates (only ammonium, potassium and sodium phosphates)
Arsenates (some)

These classes are generally soluble in acids:

Metals (gold and platinum in aqua regia)
Sulphides
Oxides (some)
Hydroxides
Fluorides
Carbonates
Borates
Silicates are mostly soluble with difficulty in boiling HF but zeolites are generally soluble in hydrochloric acid
Sulphates
Phosphates
Arsenates
Vanadates
Molybdates
Nitrates

Here are some of the more important minerals with suggestions for cleaning. Once more, leave them alone unless you know what you are doing!

Albite Oxalic or hydrochloric acids to remove iron staining; general cleaning with distilled water. Sulphuric acid will remove black stains of organic origin

Fluorite Hydrochloric acid will remove calcite coating

Garnet group Stiff wire brush or probe will remove mica encrustations; oxalic acid to remove iron stains. Chrysotile asbestos fibres may be removed by hand from demantoid crystals, notably those from Italy

Gold Iron stains removable by most acids; quartz encrustations with HF. Gold is soft so take care not to scratch specimens

Gypsum Wash off clay with water

Halite Do NOT clean with water. Use alcohol

Malachite Wash in distilled water containing a little ammonia; follow by soaking in clean water, and finally immerse in acetone. Do not use this treatment for azurmalachite

Marcasite Wash in warm distilled water, later adding ammonia. Rinse in clean water and soak in acetone to dry. Decomposing marcasite smells of sulphur

Mica group Generally acids are effective for cleaning though the lamellae may separate if water is used

Microcline feldspar Oxalic acid will remove iron stains and warm concentrated hydrochloric acid will remove hematite coating

Orpiment Use acetic acid to remove calcite encrustations

Prehnite Use hydrochloric acid to remove unwanted encrustations though it may make the surfaces powdery. Iron stains penetrating between the fibres cannot be removed

Proustite Rubbing followed by ultrasonic cleaning may get rid of the surface alteration brought about by exposure to light

Pyrite Iron stains can be removed with oxalic acid and quartz coatings with HF

Quartz Use oxalic acid to remove iron stains, hydrochloric acid to remove calcite encrustations. Do not cool quickly after immersion in warm cleaning agents

Rutile Remove other silicate coatings with HF

Silver Remove black tarnish by immersion in a solution of potassium or sodium cyanide, then in distilled water. Do not keep near sulphur-bearing substances

Sphalerite Use hydrochloric acid to remove calcite and ensure quick use to avoid dulling of faces

Spodumene HF to get rid of clay minerals which contain iron

Topaz Oxalic acid to remove iron stains, HF to remove clays

Tourmaline HF to remove clays; act quickly to avoid dulling of faces

Vanadinite Organic acids to remove calcite
Vivianite Store in the dark and in a moist atmosphere. This helps colour and mechanical stability
Willemite Pick away calcite encrustations; do not use acids

Displaying Specimens

The way in which specimens are stored must take into account their response to bright light, heat or mechanical shock. In general do not display minerals in bright light but in a subdued one; many minerals change colour after quite short exposures to bright light and others will dry out in the heat that the lights give. Try to keep temperatures constant – minerals which are heat sensitive (like sulphur) will crack if the temperature keeps on changing. Some minerals will absorb moisture from the air (halite, sylvine, ulexite) and need to be kept in sealed glass containers.

Ore minerals may develop a tarnish which may be quite attractive. Silver and copper, however, are not improved by tarnish and specimens should be kept dry and away from anything containing sulphur. Gem materials which have had their colour improved may revert to their original colour. Gemstones which have been oiled to improve their appearance may lose the oil if kept in surroundings which are too hot. Dyed stones (turquoise, lapis lazuli) may show gradual deterioration of the dye over the years.

Conserving Specimens

There should be no need today for emphasizing how important it is to preserve specimens. While many well-meaning people collect minerals and look after them quite well, in many cases they may not know precisely what they have. What appears to be one species may turn out to be quite another one, or there may be other species present whose existence was unsuspected because the equipment needed to test the specimen thoroughly was not available. Without suggesting that everyone takes everything they collect to the local museum, if the serious collector knows that the area in which he has been operating is mineralogically significant it would be well worth while having his finds checked by the local, or better, the national museum. A paper by Dunn and Mandarino in the *Mineralogical Record*, 19 (4), 1989, usefully summarizes how conservation may be advanced.

While bearing in mind that there will always be some collectors and dealers who will actually want to sell or collect rare specimens it is when type material is made the subject of rapacious collecting and commerce that science is ill-served. Type material means those specimens which have been the basis for identification of a new species or a species new to a particular locality – in fact those species about which the major papers have been written. As Dunn and Mandarino say, no mineralogical investigation is final since techniques are always improving and what was once thought may have to be modified, but it is still always valuable. What can we know of a site once it has been built upon? The early records may be the only sources here. Type specimens are the standards.

The only place for such material is in a national museum or major university collection. Such a collection must be professionally curated and its contents must be available to serious scholars who may very well be trained by the institution. Local museums and the minor universities are less acceptable homes for major specimens. In most countries this means in practice that two or three universities and the national museum are the only institutions in which type specimens can be safely deposited. Sadly in some 'developed' countries not even this minimal provision is possible. Emphasis (in the West, at least) on 'what will sell' does not usually square with scholarship and, valuable though popular button-pushing displays may be, they cannot substitute for long professional acquaintance with actual specimens. To have a display without this expertise is akin to 'liking Shakespeare' when your command of English is imperfect – you miss the finer points.

So if you are a collector, think of future generations. Many already do and this is good. Many do not and such people should ask themselves how they are enhanced by having more objects than someone else. This is a behavioural problem. Type specimens and rare minerals are sacrosanct and should always be properly housed and studied. In the long term the future of our planet depends on science taking this stand.

Keeping a Collection

There are many ways in which minerals can be stored and displayed. In general you can choose any way which best suits the accommodation you have available but it is always advisable to store specimens away from sources of strong light or heat. Questions of security also arise but, unless you have very fine and valuable specimens (particularly gemstones), housing your collection in a safe or safe deposit rather takes away an important part of keeping the specimens in the first place – the pleasure of showing them to others.

Few collectors could find the room for, or even want, museum-type display cases. Wall fittings, some of which have their own lighting, take up far less room and provided that they are not filled with ore specimens whose weight will pull them off the wall provide an excellent answer for the small or

medium-sized collection. Those who need their specimens primarily for study or lecture purposes can keep them in much less elaborate storage. Drawers intended for the storage of small tools, nuts or screws are ideal for small specimens.

Whatever type of housing you choose, you must ensure that specimens do not touch each other. They should each be contained in a lidless box within the drawer, so that when it is pulled out or pushed home the specimens will not rattle against each other. Do not put heavy specimens in the top drawers of a set or when someone unfamiliar with the collection pulls out the drawer it will fall out of control on to their head. Ensure that the material of the housing does not react unfavourably with the chemical nature of the specimens.

Above all, make sure that you keep an inventory and that it agrees with the labels on the specimens in your storage. Better still make two inventories and keep them in different places. The inventory should record the nature and size of the specimen, where it was found or from whom it was purchased or exchanged, special features and the price paid if appropriate.

Collecting in Mining Areas

It is very rare for the amateur to be allowed into a working mine for simple safety reasons and so that staff time is not taken up with visitor supervision. The collector will usually do best by prospecting the mine dumps or by keeping an eye open for civil engineering projects such as road cuts as these may open up valuable deposits.

Mines from which metallic ores are extracted will probably give the best specimens. Examples are bournite ('cog-wheel ore') from Cornwall, England, and pyrite from Panasqueira, Portugal. Fluorite from the lead mines of the English northern Pennine orefield and calcite from Cumbria, England are still sought by collectors though they are gangue minerals, that is, not those sought for processing and sale. Though at one time specimens were preserved by miners, modern mechanical methods of ore treatment do not allow for much of this as apart from the desired ores the rest is removed from the mines as slurry. Not all mines, however, are cavalier about fine crystals and a growing number, in many countries, have seen the potential for specimen sales.

Shale (Pennsylvania, USA)

Mineral Descriptions

For each species the chemical composition is given and group membership indicated. Many minerals are now known to be distinct species with strong chemical or structural links with other minerals. In these cases each species has been treated separately with the exception of the feldspars, a group whose complexity makes overall treatment easier to understand. Chemical composition follows the latest usage as listed in Fleischer's *Glossary of Mineral Species*, 5th ed., Tucson, USA, published by the *Mineralogical Record*, 1987, and its supplementary lists.

The crystal system and the commoner forms are described next. Many minerals are known to show a wide variety of forms but only those consistently reported are given here. Hardness on Mohs' scale is followed by details of cleavage where relevant. The majority of minerals display cleavage of some kind but there are considerable variations in how easy it is to start. Some minerals will cleave very easily and leave smooth surfaces behind; in such cases the cleavage is said to be perfect. Poor and indistinct are also used as descriptive terms. Some minerals with no apparent cleavage will show parting along twinning directions, as in corundum.

Specific gravity is shown next. Where the species forms part of an isomorphous series or shows a significant range of specific gravities a mean figure is sometimes given. The nature of the mineral surface, very important in field work, is given as adamantine, vitreous (glassy), pearly (usually for cleavage surfaces), resinous and so on. The colour of the majority of specimens is given with details of important variations. Diaphaneity (transparent, translucent, opaque) is also important and where a species shows a variation from one state to another the more usual one is given first.

Details of the refractive index are given for the more important minerals with possible gemstone use. Colour of streak is given where this is significant, and finally any other useful feature such as sectility, fluorescence, solubility in the commoner acids or in water, characteristic smell or feel.

Locations are given from the most up-to-date journal reports from major countries. Many species are found sparingly in some places and, while hundreds of locations could be given for quartz or feldspar minerals, only the more important ones have been included. Some locations are important for historical reasons and even though they may not be producing now they have been included. Many of those in Cornwall, England and

Wolframite (Korea)

some Alpine ones fall into this category. Spelling of place names follows current usage but country names are given in the style traditionally used by mineralogists – thus Madagascar for Malagasy Republic. Where a location is known by more than one name and both appear to have equal status the commonly accepted mineralogical one is given. In some case mine names are given where known, especially where the mine forms part of an important and extensive mining district. Details of the names of species are taken largely from Richard S. Mitchell, *Mineral Names – What Do they Mean?*, New York, Van Nostrand Reinhold, 1979.

Acanthite

Ag₂S

Bolivia

Crystal system, form and habit Monoclinic, long to short, prismatic
Hardness 2-2.5
Cleavage Poor cubic and dodecahedral
Specific gravity 7.2
Colour Iron black
Lustre Metallic
Diaphaneity Opaque
Other features Sectile
Name From Greek word for thorn, in allusion to its crystal shape

Acanthite is the stable form of Ag₂S below 177°C. Argentite is the stable form between 177°C and 586°C. Found at the Pelican Dives mine, Silver Plume district, and Little Emma mine, Clear Creek County, Colorado (USA). Also found in Canada, Mexico, Czechoslovakia, and Germany. Old specimens from Wheal Newton, Harrowbarrow, Calstock, Cornwall (England).

Actinolite

Ca₂(Mg,Fe)₅Si₈O₂₂(OH)₂

Amphibole group

Gouverneur, New York, USA

Crystal system, form and habit Monoclinic, bladed crystals frequently twinned
Hardness 5.5
Cleavage Perfect prismatic
Specific gravity 3.05
Colour Yellowish to dark green
Lustre Vitreous
Refractive index 1.619-1.644 (for transparent Tanzanian material)
Diaphaneity Transparent to translucent
Name From Greek word for ray in allusion to actinolite's fibrous nature

Actinolite forms a series with tremolite and with ferroactinolite. It occurs in contact with metamorphosed limestones and ultra-basic rocks, some material being used ornamentally. The jade

jade mineral nephrite consists largely of actinolite. Most transparent specimens from Madagascar and Tanzania; green chrome tremolite from Finland and Tanzania and light purple hexagonite from Fowler, New York (USA).

Adamite

$Zn_2(AsO_4)(OH)$

Ojuela mine, Mapimi, Mexico

Crystal system, form and habit Orthorhombic or monoclinic
Hardness 3.5

Cleavage Prismatic or dipyramidal, one direction
Specific gravity 4.48
Colour Yellowish-green or yellow
Lustre Vitreous
Refractive index 1.722-1.763
Diaphaneity Transparent to translucent
Other features Forms a series with olivenite. Dimorphous with paradamite
Name From a French mineralogist

Adamite is found in the oxidized zones of metal ore veins. Specimens from the Ojuela mine and elsewhere, Mapimi (Mexico). These are colourless, violet or pink. Also found in the slags at Laurium (Greece) where some specimens show a yellowish-green fluorescence. Copper-coloured specimens (pink and green) from Cap Garonne (France). The copper green is especially fine in crystals from Tsumeb (Namibia) where the best specimens are translucent. Recently crystals have been reported from Gansu (China). In general adamite crystals are found in cavities in limonite.

Almandine

$Fe_3Al_2(SiO_4)_3$

Garnet group

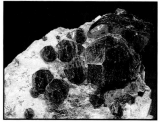

Southbury, Connecticut, USA

Crystal system, form and habit Cubic, forming rhombic dodecahedra, icositetrahedra or combinations; sometimes formless lumps

Hardness 7-7.5
Specific gravity 4.1-4.3
Colour Deep blood-red, brownish-red
Lustre Vitreous to resinous
Refractive index 1.830
Streak White
Diaphaneity Transparent
Other features Forms an isomorphous series with pyrope; strong absorption band at 505nm distinguishes from other red transparent minerals
Name From Alabanda (Asia Minor), thought to be an early centre for garnet fashioning

Almandine is found in schists, gneisses and other metamorphic rocks and is extensively used as a gemstone, being cut as a hollow cabochon to avoid too black an appearance. Most gem almandine comes from India or Sri Lanka. Fine crystals are found at Wrangell (Alaska) and in the Emerald Creek district, Benewah County, Idaho (USA).

Amblygonite

(Li,Na)Al(PO₄)(F,OH)

Amblygonite group

Brazil

Crystal system, form and habit Triclinic forming equant to

short prismatic crystals
Hardness 5-5.6
Cleavage Perfect basal
Specific gravity 3-3.1
Colour Clear lemon yellow
Lustre Vitreous or pearly
Refractive index 1.578-1.612
Diaphaneity Transparent
Other features May show weak orange fluorescence LWUV
Name From Greek word alluding to the bluntness of the crystal

Amblygonite forms a series with montebrasite and was once a source of lithium. Found in granite pegmatites, the best faceting material coming from Arassuahy (Brazil). Most faceted stones are montebrasite which has a specific gravity of 2.98.

Analcime $NaAlSi_2O_6.H_2O$

Zeolite group

Frombach, Italian Tirol

Crystal system, form and habit Cubic, often found as icositetrahedra

Hardness 5-5.5

Cleavage Cubic in traces
Specific gravity 2.22-2.29
Colour Colourless, white, sometimes with yellow or pink tinges from impurities
Refractive index 1.487
Diaphaneity Transparent to translucent
Other features Forms a series with pollucite
Name From Greek word meaning weak, referring to a weak electrical charge developed on rubbing

Occurs as a secondary mineral in basic igneous rocks. Worldwide occurrence but notable crystals from Mont St Hilaire, Québec (Canada), Orkney and Faroe Islands, Fassa Valley, Tirol (Austria), St Andreasberg, Harz Mountains (West Germany), Antronapiana, Ossola, Novara (Italy), from the New Jersey traprocks at Paterson (USA).

Anatase TiO_2

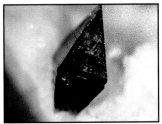

El Dorado, Montgomery County, USA

Crystal system, form and habit Tetragonal, steeply pyramidal, octahedral or tabular, often complex

Hardness 5.5-6

Cleavage Perfect basal and pyramidal
Specific gravity 3.8-3.9
Colour Blue, yellow or brown
Lustre Adamantine to sub-metallic
Diaphaneity Transparent to translucent
Other features Polymorphous with rutile and brookite
Name From Greek word meaning extension, alluding to the longer common pyramid form shown in comparison with other minerals of the tetragonal system

Anatase is found in Alpine veins, often on rock crystal. Finest examples come from central Switzerland, especially from the Binntal, Tavetsch and St Gotthard. Also from Baceno, Valle Antigorio, Novara (Italy), and from Norway. Small deep blue transparent crystals from diamond washings in Minas Gerais (Brazil).

Andalusite

Al_2SiO_5

Lüsens, Tirol, Austria

Crystal system, form and habit Orthorhombic, crystals are square prisms but much ornamental material found as water-worn pebbles

Hardness 6.5-7.5
Cleavage Distinct prismatic
Specific gravity 3.13-3.17
Colour Dark green with strong pleochroism giving flesh-red colour
Lustre Vitreous
Refractive index 1.629-1.650
Diaphaneity Transparent, translucent or opaque
Other features Polymorphous with sillimanite and kyanite
Name From Andalucia (Spain), an early but now unimportant location

Andalusite is a characteristic mineral of metamorphic rocks, especially gneisses, slates and schists. The variety chiastolite occurs as long brown opaque crystals with black carbonaceous cross-like inclusions visible in cross-section. Most gem-quality material comes from Brazil where golden-yellow crystals have recently been found. Also from the Fichtelgebirge (West Germany), Lüsens, Tirol (Austria), Mursinka (USSR), Mt Howden (Australia). The best chiastolite comes from Santiago de Compostela (Spain).

Andradite

$Ca_3Fe_2(SiO_4)_3$

Crystal system, form and habit Cubic, forming rhombic dodecahedra, icositetrahedra or combinations
Hardness 6.5-7
Specific gravity 3.7-4.1
Colour Yellowish to emerald green, black
Lustre Vitreous
Refractive index 1.89

Found most commonly in chlorite schists and in serpentines. Fine emerald-green transparent material used as gemstones and known as demantoid, referring to the high lustre. These crystals come from the Sysert district of the Ural Mountains (USSR). Crystals of a yellower-green from the Ala valley, Piedmont (Italy). Fine yellow-orange crystals from Serifos (Greece) and well-formed brown specimens from Emmelberg, Eifel (West Germany). Andradite is also found at Banat (Romania), Italian Mountain, Colorado (USA), and from Shanxi (China). Forms a series with grossular.

Anglesite $PbSO_4$

Barite group

Touissit, Morocco

Crystal system, form and habit Orthorhombic, usually thick tabular

Hardness 2.5-3
Cleavage Basal and prismatic
Specific gravity 6.38
Colour Colourless to white or grey; brown
Lustre Adamantine inclining to resinous
Refractive index 1.877-1.894
Streak Colourless
Diaphaneity Transparent to translucent
Other features Weak yellow to orange fluorescence LWUV
Name From Anglesey (Wales)

Anglesite is formed by the oxidation of galena and is found in lead ore deposits as a secondary mineral. Some stones of an attractive orange-brown or light-yellow are transparent enough to be faceted. These come from Touissit (Morocco). Fine crystals are found in Sardinia at Monteponi and Montevecchio, and at Tavetsch (Switzerland), Derbyshire (England). The Coeur d'Alene district of Idaho (USA), Tsumeb (Namibia), and Broken Hill, New South Wales (Australia) also provide good quality crystals. In many occurrences anglesite is found with minute yellow sulphur crystals on galena which has been altered.

Anhydrite

$CaSO_4$

Switzerland

Crystal system, form and habit Orthorhombic, thin tabular though rare crystals, commonly massive
Hardness 3.5
Cleavage 3 pinacoidal
Specific gravity 2.98

Colour colourless, grey, pale shades of blue, violet, red and brown
Lustre Vitreous to greasy
Refractive index 1.56-1.61
Streak White
Diaphaneity Transparent to translucent
Other features May fluoresce different colours on heating: blue-white (Swiss), yellow-green (New Jersey)
Name From Greek word meaning 'without water' in comparison with gypsum, the water-bearing and commoner calcium sulphate

An important rock-forming mineral associated with gypsum, salt beds, dolomite or limestone. It is found in hydrothermal vein deposits and cavities in igneous trap rock. Strata in western South Dakota, Carlsbad, New Mexico (USA); zeolites in cavities in igneous rocks in New Jersey, Massachusetts and New York (USA). Fine specimens at the Faraday uranium mine, Bancroft, Ontario (Canada). In salt deposits of Germany, in particular Stassfurt (East Germany), Austria, Wieliczka (Poland), France, India. Fine crystals have been encountered while drilling at the Simplon Tunnel (Switzerland); also from Campione, Grosset (Italy).

Ankerite

$Ca(Fe^{2+},Mg,Mn)(CO_3)_2$

Eagle mine, Colorado, USA
Crystal system, form and

habit Trigonal, simple rhombohedrons, twinning common
Hardness 3.5-4
Cleavage 1 perfect
Specific gravity 2.97
Colour White or grey to yellowish-brown or brown
Lustre Vitreous to pearly
Refractive index 1.72-1.53
Name From Matthias Joseph Anker, Austrian mineralogist

Ankerite is found with gold at the Homestake mine, South Dakota (USA), and in sulphide veins in the Coeur d'Alene area of Idaho (USA). Also in the Oldham area, Lancashire (England), and at Erzberg, Styria (Austria).

Apophyllite

$KCa_4Si_8O_{20}(F,OH)·_8H_2O$

Poona, India

Crystal system, form and habit Tetragonal, pseudocubic

crystals
Hardness 4.5-5
Cleavage Perfect basal
Specific gravity 2.3-2.5
Colour White; pale to medium green
Lustre Vitreous to pearly
Refractive index 1.534-1.537
Diaphaneity Transparent to translucent
Name From a Greek word referring to the mineral's tendency to exfoliate on heating

Apophyllite occurs as a secondary mineral in basic igneous rocks, chiefly as large pale green crystals in the area of Bombay, particularly at the Pashan quarries, Khadaksvala, Poona (India). Also from the traprocks at Paterson, New Jersey (USA), and as fine crystals on prehnite at Fairfax, Virginia (USA). Delicate pink crystals are sometimes found at the deposits in the Harz Mountains (West Germany), and Guanajuato (Mexico). Also reported from Liaoning and Fujian (China).

Aragonite

$CaCO_3$

Aragonite group

Tazouta, Morocco

Crystal system, form and habit Orthorhombic, pseudohexagonal crystals, frequently twinned
Hardness 3.5-4
Cleavage Poor
Specific gravity 2.93-2.95
Colour Colourless; light blue to violet; yellow
Refractive index 1.53-1.685
Diaphaneity Translucent to

transparent
Other features Effervesces in
HCl. Some Sicilian material may
luminesce green LWUV
Name From Molina de Aragon
(Spain)

Aragonite is dimorphous with calcite and is found in hot spring
deposits, ore veins and sedimentary rocks. Straw-yellow crystals
of gem quality are found at Horschenz (West Germany) and at
Erzberg, Styria and Hüttenberg (Austria). Other important
European sources include Karlovy Vary (Czechoslovakia) and
Agrigento (Sicily) with pale blue crystals coming from the slags
at Laurium (Greece) and near-colourless crystals from
Minglanilla (Spain). Violet rod-like crystals occur in gas cavities
in basalt at Suzu Gun, Ishikawa prefecture (Japan).

Argentite

Ag_2S

Silver Center, Cobalt, Ontario, Canada

**Crystal system, form and
habit** Cubic; cubes or octahedra;
usually massive, branching,
reticulated; interpenetrant twins
common
Hardness 2.5-3.5
Cleavage Poor, cubic and
dodecahedral
Specific gravity 7.2-7.3
Colour Lead grey to black
Lustre Metallic
Diaphaneity Opaque
Other features Very sectile
Stable only above 177°C
Name From Latin argentum
(silver)

Argentite is dimorphous with acanthite and occurs in
moderately low temperature sulphide ore deposits. It is
associated with native silver and galena and is found in western
USA, particularly in the Comstock Lode, Nevada. Fine crystals
also occur in silver districts of Mexico, Germany,
Czechoslovakia, Sardinia and Norway.

Arsenopyrite

FeAsS

Arsenopyrite group

Santa Eulalia, Mexico

Crystal system, form and

habit Monoclinic, elongated, pseudo-orthorhombic; massive
Hardness 5.5-6
Cleavage Prismatic
Specific gravity 5.9-6.2
Colour Silver-white
Lustre Metallic
Streak Black
Diaphaneity Opaque
Other features Garlic smell on fracture
Name From its composition

Arsenopyrite is most commonly found in high-temperature veins, sometimes in pegmatites. Good crystals from the nickel-silver mines at Freiberg (East Germany) and from the metalliferous mining areas of south-west England, in particular from Wheal Penrose, Sithney, Cornwall, and the Virtuous Lady mine, Buckland Monachorum, Devon. Also from the tin mines of Bolivia and from Panasqueira (Portugal), Cinovec (Czechoslovakia), and Montevecchio, Sardinia (Italy). Crystals have been reported also from Cobalt, Ontario (Canada), Mother Lode, California (USA) and Hunan (China).

Atacamite

$Cu_2Cl(OH)_3$

Burra Burra, Australia

Crystal system, form and

habit Orthorhombic, slender, prismatic or tabular; twinned; masses
Hardness 3-3.5
Cleavage 1 perfect
Specific gravity 3.76
Colour Bright green to blackish-green
Lustre Vitreous to adamantine
Streak Apple-green
Diaphaneity Transparent
Name From the location

Atacamite is found as a secondary mineral in the oxidation zone of copper deposits. From Cornwall, (England); Goffs, San Bernardino County, California (USA); Tintic district, Juab County, Utah (USA). From Boleo and El Toro, Baja

California, (Mexico); Wallaroo (Australia); Tsumeb (Namibia); Atacama desert (Chile); Rheinbreitbach (West Germany), and especially from Mina la Farola, Copiapo (Chile).

Augelite

$Al_2PO_4(OH)_3$

Hardness 4.5-5
Cleavage 2 good
Specific gravity 2.7
Colour Colourless, yellow, pale blue
Lustre Vitreous, pearly on cleavage
Refractive index 1.57-1.58
Streak White
Diaphaneity Transparent to translucent

Location unknown
Crystal system, form and habit Monoclinic, thick tabular, prismatic to acicular, thin triangular plates or massive

Name From Greek word for lustre in allusion to its pearly cleavage surfaces

Augelite is found as transparent colourless crystals at White Mountain, Mono County, California (USA) in an andalusite ore body. Small crystals associated with lazulite, albite and quartz are found at the Smith mine, Newport and at the Palermo mine, North Groton, New Hampshire (USA). Also from Bolivia and Sweden.

Augite

$(Ca,Na)(Mg,Fe,Al)(Si,Al,Ti)_2O_6$

Pyroxene group

Hardness 5.5-6
Cleavage Perfect prismatic at 87°C
Specific gravity 3.23-3.52
Colour Pale to dark brown, green or black, purple-brown
Lustre Vitreous to dull
Refractive index 1.67-1.76
Streak Greyish-green
Diaphaneity Translucent on edges

Otter Lake, Quebec, Canada
Crystal system, form and habit Monoclinic; stout prisms often twinned; massive

Name From Greek word for lustre, alluding to its cleavage surfaces

Augite occurs as a constituent of basalts, dolerites and gabbros. There are many occurrences worldwide. Fine crystals from Monte Somma, Vesuvius (Italy); Kaiserstuhl (West Germany); Nordmarkgrund, Vermland (Sweden); Schwarzenstein, Zillertal and Hohe Tauern (Austria); Fassa valley, Piedmont (Italy); the Binntal, Valais (Switzerland).

Aurichalcite

$(Zn,Cu)_5(CO_3)_2(OH)_6$

Kelly, New Mexico, USA

Crystal system, form and habit Orthorhombic giving crusts of scales
Hardness 2
Cleavage Micaceous
Specific gravity 3.5-3.6
Colour Pale greenish-blue
Lustre Pearly
Diaphaneity Translucent
Name From Greek for copper or Latin for gold (it does not contain gold nor resemble it)

Aurichalcite is formed by the weathering of zinc-rich ore bodies. It forms soft crusts on limonite. From Leadhills, Lanarkshire (Scotland); Matlock, Derbyshire (England); from copper mines in Arizona and New Mexico (USA); Altai region (USSR); Yugoslavia; Chessy (France); Laurium (Greece).

Autunite

$Ca(UO_2)_2(PO_4)_2.10-12H_2O$

Autunite group

Spokane, Washington, USA
Crystal system, form and habit Tetragonal, found in square plates or thin micaceous

flakes or crusts with crystals on the edges
Hardness 2-2.5
Cleavage Perfect basal and prismatic
Specific gravity 3.1
Colour Greenish-yellow
Lustre Pearly to vitreous
Diaphaneity Translucent
Other features Very bright green fluorescence in ultraviolet light
Name From Autun (France)

Autunite is found abundantly in weathered zones of ore deposits and in uranium-bearing pegmatites, especially at Spruce Pine, North Carolina (USA), and at Mount Painter, (Australia), and Urgeiriça (Portugal). Rich greenish crusts from Saône-et-Loire and Margnac, Haute-Vienne (France).

Axinite

$(Ca,Mn,Fe,Mg)_2Al_2BSi_4O_{15}(OH)$

Axinite group

New Melones Lake, California, USA

Crystal system, form and habit Triclinic, distinctive wedge-shape
Hardness 6.5-7

Cleavage 1 good, several poor
Specific gravity 3.26-3.36
Colour Cinnamon-brown, olive-green, reddish-purple, violet, yellow, colourless with strong pleochroism
Lustre Vitreous
Refractive index 1.674-1.668
Diaphaneity Transparent to translucent
Other features Some material may fluoresce red
Name From Greek word referring to crystal shape

Axinite is found in areas of contact metamorphism and metasomatism. Most gem quality material comes from Baja California (Mexico). Fine crystals found at St Christophe, Bourg d'Oisans, Hautes-Alpes (France); abundant in the granites of south-western England, particularly from the Stamps and Jowl Zawn, Roscommon Cliff, St Just, Cornwall. Recently reported from the Schächental, Uri (Switzerland) and from Miage, Aosta (Italy). Red-fluorescent manganese-rich material from Franklin, New Jersey (USA). Axinite also comes from Vitoria da Conquista, Bahia (Brazil) and from Luning, Nevada (USA).

Azurite

$Cu_3(CO_3)_2(OH)_2$

Bisbee, Arizona, USA

Crystal system, form and habit Monoclinic, large tabular, more commonly as rosettes or masses often intimately associated with malachite (azur-malachite)
Hardness 3.5-4
Cleavage 1 good, 2 poor
Specific gravity 3.77
Colour Deep blue
Lustre Vitreous
Refractive index 1.73-1.836
Diaphaneity Transparent in thin pieces
Other features Dissolves in HCl with effervescence
Name From its colour

Azurite is found as a secondary mineral in copper deposits. From Altenmittlau, Spessart (West Germany); fine crystals from Chessy (France); from Rudabanya (Hungary) and the Eifel region of West Germany; Tynagh mine (Ireland). Small gem-quality crystals found at Tsumeb (Namibia) and fine coloured masses from Arizona (USA) locations, particularly Bisbee and the New Cornelia mine, Ajo. The Copper Queen mine at Bisbee is one of the world's most famous azurite locations.

Barite

$BaSO_4$

Barite group

Elk Creek, South Dakota, USA

Crystal system, form and habit Orthorhombic, thick to thin tabular; well-formed crystals common
Hardness 3-3.5
Cleavage Perfect basal and prismatic
Specific gravity 4.5
Colour Colourless, white, yellow-brown to blue
Lustre Vitreous to resinous
Refractive index 1.63-1.64
Streak White
Diaphaneity Transparent to translucent
Other features Some varieties fluoresce orange LWUV; frequently coloured by inclusions of hematite or sulphides
Name From Greek words meaning weight and heavy

The old name for barite is 'heavy spar' and the high SG is useful as a field test. The commonest ore of barium, it is found in hydrothermal veins or sedimentary rocks such as limestones. Fluorite, quartz or galena often occur in association. A great many occurrences worldwide provide fine crystals; some of the best known are Alston Moor, Cleator Moor, and Frizington (England) and several places in Cornwall, particularly Wheal Mary Ann mine at Menheniot. In Europe good crystals come from Freiberg and Marienberg, Saxony (East Germany), and from Drieslar, Sauerland, Grube Clara, Schwarzwald (West Germany). Also from Grube Machow, Tarnobrzeg (Poland) where the mineral occurs as attractive yellow crystals and from Monteveglio, Bologna (Italy) and from the Limagne district, Puy-de-Dôme (France). Some barite is found in Castile and Andalucia (Spain). The famous mining district of Pribram (Czechoslovakia) provides good crystals and barite occurs with stibnite needles at Baia Sprie – formerly Felsobanya (Romania). Fine blue crystals occur at Sterling, Colorado and gem-quality yellow crystals from Elk Creek, South Dakota (USA). Also from the USA are fine yellow plates from the Magma mine, Arizona. Sand-bearing 'desert roses' are found in Oklahoma and brown crystals with vicinal faces occurring in cavities in concretions and fossils from the Bad Lands of South Dakota. Recently crystals have been reported from Sichuan and Guangxi (China).

Bayldonite $PbCu_3(AsO_4)_2(OH)_2.H_2O$

Tsumeb, Namibia

Crystal system, form and habit Monoclinic, mamillary concretions
Hardness 4.5
Specific gravity 5.5
Colour Apple to yellow-green
Lustre Resinous
Refractive index 1.95-1.99
Name From John Bayldon

Bayldonite is found as a secondary mineral in the oxidized zone of copper deposits. It was first identified from St Day, Cornwall, and from Penberthy Crofts, St Just (England). It occurs with mimetite, olivenite and other arsenates and is found at Tsumeb (Namibia), Knappengrund, Münstertal and Grube Clara, Schwarzwald (West Germany).

Benitoite

BaTiSi$_3$O$_9$

San Benito County, California, USA
Crystal system, form and habit Hexagonal, distinctive

flattened pyramids
Hardness 6.6.5
Cleavage Poor pyramidal
Specific gravity 3.64-3.68
Colour Blue, rarely pink
Lustre Vitreous
Refractive index 1.75-1.8
Diaphaneity Transparent
Other features Intense blue fluorescence SWUV
Name From San Benito County, California (USA)

Used as a gemstone when sufficiently transparent, benitoite is found in San Benito County, California (USA), where it occurs with the rare minerals joaquinite and neptunite in a matrix of white natrolite. It also occurs as six-sided blue crystals at Omi Machi, Nishi-Kubiki Gun, Niigata prefecture (Japan), and as grains in some Belgian rocks. When faceted it is extremely beautiful.

Beryl

Be$_3$Al$_2$(SiO$_3$)$_6$

Brazil
Crystal system, form and habit Hexagonal, forming

hexagonal prisms
Hardness 7.5-8
Cleavage
Specific gravity 2.6-2.9
Colour Yellow, golden yellow, blue, pale to emerald green, pink, red, colourless
Lustre Vitreous
Refractive index 1.566-1.594
Name From Greek beryllos, a word applied at various times to different green minerals

Beryl occurs in granite pegmatites, in biotite schists and in pneumatolytic hydrothermal veins. The most valuable beryl is emerald which is coloured by chromium; the most famous localities are Chivor and Muzo (Colombia), Pakistan, Zimbabwe, the Ural Mountains (USSR), various localities in Brazil, the Habachtal (Austria). Included minerals often make it possible to place the origin of a transparent emerald. Other varieties of beryl include aquamarine which is a fine blue and is found in Brazil. Especially fine crystals occur at mines in the Teofilo Otoni area of Minas Gerais (Brazil). Aquamarine is also found in the Sawtooth Mountains, Idaho (USA). The golden beryl which shades into yellow is also found at Brazilian locations and very fine deep crystals are found in Namibia and in the Urals. Pink beryl, known as morganite, is characteristic of some Madagascar pegmatites and is found particularly at Anjanabonoina. Morganite is also found in San Diego County, California (USA) and in Brazil. Rare but fine transparent small red crystals of a manganese-bearing beryl are found in a rhyolite in the Wah Wah Mountains of Utah (USA). Green (non-emerald) beryl is found in a number of places. Some contains vanadium and is an attractive bright apple-green and occurs in Brazil. Green beryl also comes from Altay, Xingjiang (China), Wolodarsk-Wolynsky, Wolyn, Ukraine (USSR), Orissa (India) and Böckstein (Austria). Beryl in light colours has also been reported from Nigeria, and from Piz Badile, Ticino (Switzerland), Drammen (Norway), Ober-Mengelbach, Odenwald, Hesse (West Germany).

Betafite $(Ca,Na,U)_2(Ti,Nb,Ta)_2O_6(OH)$

Pyrochlore group

Silver Crater, Ontario, Canada

Crystal system, form and habit Cubic, prismatic, elongated, sometimes flattened
Hardness 2.5-3
Cleavage 1 perfect
Specific gravity 3.9
Colour Black, brown, yellow
Lustre Waxy, submetallic, vitreous
Name Named from Betafo (Madagascar)

Betafite is found with zircon in pegmatites, biotite and beryl often accompanying it. Fine crystals occur in the Silver Crater mine, Bancroft, Ontario (Canada) and at a number of mines in Colorado (USA).

Biotite

$K(Mg,Fe^{2+})_3(Al,Fe^{3+})Si_3O_{10}(OH,F)_2$

Mica group

Ontario, Canada

Crystal system, form and habit Monoclinic, usually massive, scaly, twinned

Hardness 2.5-3
Cleavage Perfect basal
Specific gravity 2.7-3.4
Colour Black, brown, reddish-brown or green
Lustre Splendent, near submetallic, vitreous or pearly
Refractive index 1.56-1.69
Streak Colourless
Diaphaneity Opaque to translucent
Name From French physicist Jean Baptiste Biot

Biotite has a worldwide occurrence in granites, pegmatites, gabbros, schists, gneisses and other rocks. Well-developed crystals can be found at Somma, Vesuvius (Italy), Monte Albani (Italy), Laacher See, Eifel (West Germany), and Xinjiang (China).

Bismuth

Bi

Arsenic group

Patosi, Bolivia

Crystal system, form and

habit Trigonal, usually ill-formed
Hardness 2-2.5
Cleavage Perfect
Specific gravity 9.7-9.83
Colour Silver-white reddish hue
Lustre Metallic, iridescent tarnish
Other features Fine hopper crystals characteristic of artificial product only
Name Perhaps from Greek word meaning lead-white

Bismuth is found in hydrothermal veins with cobalt ores and those of silver, nickel and tin. It is found especially in Saxony, (East Germany), in the Schneeberg and Johanngeorgenstadt areas of the Erzgebirge (East Germany), at Ossola, Novara (Italy), at St Just, St Ives and Camborne, Cornwall (England) and at several localities in Norway and Sweden.

Bismuthinite

Bi_2S_3

Mt Moly, Queensland, Australia

Crystal system, form and

habit Orthorhombic, stout prismatic to acicular, striated
Hardness 2
Cleavage Perfect side pinacoid
Specific gravity 6.78
Colour Lead grey to white
Lustre Metallic
Streak Lead grey
Other features Yellowish or iridescent tarnish; slightly sectile
Name From its composition

Bismuthinite is found in high-temperature hydrothermal veins associated with bismuth, quartz and sulphides. It sometimes occurs in granite pegmatites and in tin deposits. Found at Schneeberg, Saxony (East Germany); Rezbanya (Romania); in England at Redruth, Cornwall, at the Fowey Consols mine, St Blazey, at Tavistock, Devon, and at Carrock Fell, Cumbria. There are fine deposits at Llallagua (Bolivia). It occurs with chrysoberyl at Haddam, Connecticut (USA) and in the Granite mining area of Beaver County, Colorado (USA). Also found in Guangdong (China).

Boleite

$Pb_{26}Ag_{10}Cu_{24}Cl_{62}(OH)_{48}.3H_2O$

Boleo, Baja California, Mexico

Crystal system, form and habit Cubic
Hardness 3-3.5
Cleavage 1 perfect
Specific gravity 5.05
Colour Deep blue to indigo
Lustre Vitreous to pearly
Refractive index 2.03-2.05
Streak Blue with greenish tinge
Name From the locality

Found with other secondary lead minerals at Boleo and the Amelia mine, Santa Rosalia, Baja California (Mexico).

Boracite

$Mg_3B_7O_{13}Cl$

Lüneburg, West Germany

Crystal system, form and habit Orthorhombic, pseudocubic, dodecahedral
Hardness 7-7.5
Specific gravity 2.95
Colour Colourless, yellow, pale to dark green
Lustre Vitreous
Refractive index 1.65-1.67
Name From borax

Found in rock salt masses which are not soluble in water. Occurs at the Choctaw salt dome, Iberville, Louisiana (USA); Aislaby, Yorkshire (England); Luneville, La Meurthe (France). Many fine crystals in halite beds in the Stassfurt and Hanover areas of Germany in particular.

Borax

$Na_2B_4O_5(OH)_4.8H_2O$

Boron, California, USA

Crystal system, form and habit Monoclinic, sometimes giving very large well-formed crystals or occurring as crusts
Hardness 2-2.5
Cleavage 3 directions, 1 good
Specific gravity 1.7
Colour White, yellowish, grey, bluish, greenish or colourless
Diaphaneity Transparent to translucent
Other features Turns white as water is lost. Tastes bitter-sweet
Name From the Persian burah and Arabic buraq, former names for the mineral

Found in dry lake beds in deserts; found and worked from Searles Lake, California (USA).

Bornite

Cu$_5$FeS$_4$

Butte, Montana, USA

Hardness 3
Cleavage Poor octahedral
Specific gravity 5.06-5.08
Colour Red to brown, purple when tarnished
Lustre Metallic
Streak Pale grey-black
Other features Reddish-brown on fresh surfaces and purplish iridescent on fresh fractures
Name From Ignatius von Born, Austrian mineralogist. Mineral known as 'peacock ore' from its tarnish colours

Crystal system, form and habit Cubic, dodecahedral, forming typical penetration twins; usually massive

In general crystals are rare but are found in major copper deposits. Crystals occur at Carn Brea, Redruth, Cornwall (England); Vohemar (Madagascar); from Pragratten and Winisch-Matrei, Tirol (Austria); at Bristol, Connecticut and Butte, Montana (USA); spinel twins from Naica (Mexico). From Frossnitz (Austria), and at Tsumeb (Namibia).

Boulangerite

Pb$_5$Sb$_4$S$_{11}$

Silver King mine, Park City, Utah, USA

Crystal system, form and habit Monoclinic, long prismatic or fibrous crystals, also massive
Hardness 2.5-3
Cleavage Good cleavage, parallel to elongation
Specific gravity 5.7-6.3
Colour Bluish lead-grey
Lustre Metallic
Other features Flexible
Name From Charles Louis Boulanger, a french mining engineer

Found in veins with other lead sulphosalts; hair-like crystals from a number of locations including Trepca (Yugoslavia) and Zacatecas (Mexico); feathery masses from Stevens County, Washington (USA). Fibres more brittle than those of jamesonite which they resemble. Also from Ramsbeck, Sauerland (West Germany); Guangxi (China).

Bournonite

PbCuSbS₃

West Germany
Crystal system, form and

habit Orthorhombic, forming characteristic intergrown cog-wheel crystals.
Hardness 2.5-3
Cleavage Good cleavage one direction; 2 less good at 90° to it
Specific gravity 5.8-5.9
Colour Black to greyish-black
Lustre Metallic to adamantine
Name From the French crystallographer Jacques Louis de Bournon

Found in cavities in medium-temperature ore veins associated with galena, sphalerite, tetrahedrite and quartz. Fine examples from Herodsfoot mine, Cornwall (England); Neudorf, Harz Mountains (West Germany); Horhausen, Rhein (West Germany); the Chichubu mine, Saitama prefecture (Japan); Utah (USA); Broken Hill, New South Wales (Australia); and from Sonora (Mexico).

Brazilianite

NaAl₃(PO₄)₂(OH)₄

Minas Gerais, Brazil
Crystal system, form and

habit Monoclinic, short prismatic or near-equant
Hardness 5.5
Cleavage 1 perfect
Specific gravity 2.98
Colour Yellowish-green
Lustre Vitreous
Refractive index 1.60-1.62
Streak Colourless
Diaphaneity Transparent to translucent
Name From the major locality

Found in pegmatites as a result of hydrothermal deposition. Occurs in cavities at the Palermo mine, Grafton County, New Hampshire (USA) and at the Smith mine in the same state. Very fine crystals from the Corrego Frio mine, Divino das Laranjeiras (Brazil).

Brookite

TiO$_2$

Magnet Cove, Arkansas, USA

Cleavage Poor prismatic and basal
Specific gravity 3.87-4.14
Colour Yellowish-brown to brown or dark orange
Lustre Subadamantine
Refractive index 2.5-2.7
Diaphaneity Translucent to opaque
Other features Strongly pleochroic. Polymorphous with rutile and anatase
Name From J H Brooke, English mineralogist

Crystal system, form and habit Orthorhombic, tabular or prismatic striated crystals
Hardness 5.5-6

A characteristic Alpine-deposit mineral, occurring in schists and gneisses as well as in igneous rocks. Deposits include Prägraten, Tirol, and Ankogelgebiet, Hohe Tauern (Austria); Amsteg and Iragana in the Ticino (Switzerland). Also found at Bourg d'Oisans, (France); formerly from a quartz vein at Tremadoc (Wales) and from Magnet Cove, Arkansas (USA).

Bustamite

(Mn,Ca)$_3$Si$_3$O$_9$

Honshu, Japan

and rounded
Hardness 5.5-6.5
Cleavage Perfect 1 direction
Specific gravity 3.32-3.43
Colour Pale pink to orange- or brownish-red
Lustre Vitreous
Refractive index 1.662-1.707
Diaphaneity Transparent to translucent
Name From the Mexican General, Anastasio Bustamente

Crystal system, form and habit Triclinic; crystals usually tabular

Bustamite is found in manganese ore bodies, often with rhodonite which it closely resembles. Fine coloured crystals from Iwate and Yamagata prefectures (Japan); also from Broken Hill, New South Wales (Australia); Langban (Sweden); Meldon, Devon (England).

Cacoxenite $(Fe^{3+},Al)_{25}(PO_4)_{17}O_6(OH)_{12}.75H_2O$

Leveaniemi mine, Svappavara, Sweden

Crystal system, form and habit Hexagonal, crystals minute and acicular; usually as tufted aggregates or crusts
Hardness 3-4
Specific gravity 2.26
Colour Golden to yellow or brownish
Lustre Silky
Name From Greek words meaning bad guest, alluding to the harmful effect of the phosphorus on the iron found in the limonite in which the cacoxenite also occurs

Found as a secondary mineral with other phosphates and with limonite. From the Eleonore mine, Giessen and from localities in Bavaria, notably Hagendorf, (West Germany); from the Leveaniemi mine, Svappavara (Sweden).

Calcite $CaCO_3$

Derbyshire, England

Crystal system, form and habit Trigonal with a great number of recorded forms, frequently twinned
Hardness 3
Cleavage Perfect rhombohedral
Specific gravity 2.71-2.94
Colour Many pale colours
Lustre Vitreous, pearly on cleavages
Refractive index 1.4-1.7
Diaphaneity Transparent to translucent
Other features Many different luminescent effects. Dissolves with effervescence in cold HCl
Name From the Latin word for lime

Calcite is polymorphous with aragonite and occurs in almost every type of environment, worldwide. The name alabaster should be reserved for gypsum. The marble form of calcite is used ornamentally. Fine crystals from a number of localities, including St Andreasberg, Harz (West Germany), Egremont, Cumbria (England) and from Wheal Wrey, Liskeard, Cornwall (England); from Missouri (USA) in large crystals; large clear

'Iceland spar' from Helgustedir, Eskifjord (Iceland). The pink variety sphaerocobaltite contains cobalt as the name suggests.

Caledonite

$Pb_5Cu_2(CO_3)(SO_4)_3(OH)_6$

Susanna mine, Leadhills, Scotland

Crystal system, form and habit Orthorhombic, small well-formed crystals
Hardness 2.5-3
Cleavage 1 good 2 poor
Specific gravity 5.8
Colour Light blue to blue-green
Lustre Resinous
Diaphaneity Translucent
Name From Caledonia, the old name for Scotland

Found in the weathered zone of lead and copper ore deposits. Fine micromount specimens from the Mammoth mine, Tiger, Arizona (USA), and from Scotland, Montevecchio, Sardinia (Italy), and Chile.

Cassiterite

SnO_2

Rutile group

Pinos, Mexico

Cleavage Poor prismatic
Specific gravity 6.99
Colour Yellowish-brown to dark brown
Lustre Adamantine to metallic; greasy on fracture surfaces
Refractive index 2.0-2.1
Streak White or brownish
Diaphaneity Transparent to translucent
Other features Often shows colour zoning; high dispersion of 0.071
Name From the Greek word for tin

Crystal system, form and habit Tetragonal, commonly twinned or as short or long prismatic
Hardness 6-7

Cassiterite is the chief ore of tin and occurs in medium to high-temperature veins, in metasomatic deposits, granite pegmatites and rhyolites. Much cassiterite is found alluvially. Fine crystals from the Araca mine (Bolivia) have been faceted. There are several locations in Saxony (East Germany) and in Czechoslovakia and Cornwall (England), notably the Prideaux Wood mine, Luxulyan, Dolcoath mine, Camborne; wood tin from the West Kitty mine, St Agnes (England). The variety wood tin is found in botryoidal or reniform masses with a concentric structure, a radial fibrous interior and brown colour. Cassiterite has not proved economically viable in the USA. Tin placers in many localities, particularly in Nigeria, Malaysia, Bolivia, and Brazil.

Cavansite

$Ca(VO)Si_4O_{10}·4H_2O$

Poona, India

Crystal system, form and habit Orthorhombic, prismatic or forming spherulitic rosettes
Hardness 3-4
Cleavage Good
Specific gravity 2.32
Colour Brilliant greenish-blue
Lustre Vitreous
Diaphaneity Transparent
Name From its composition

Found with calcite and some zeolites in the Poona area (India) and from the Chapman quarry, Goble, Columbia County, Oregon (USA)

Celestine

$SrSO_4$

Barite group

Sicily

Crystal system, form and habit Orthorhombic, forming tabular crystals
Hardness 3-3.5
Cleavage Perfect basal and prismatic; poor pinacoidal
Specific gravity 3.97-4.00
Colour Colourless, some pale blue
Lustre Vitreous, pearly on cleavage surfaces
Refractive index 1.62-1.63
Streak White
Diaphaneity Transparent to translucent

Other features Blue fluorescence SWUV; may phosphoresce blue-white

Name From the Latin for 'celestial' from the blue colour

Celestine occurs in sedimentary rocks, particularly in limestones, or in hydrothermal vein deposits and igneous rocks. Faceted stones are sometimes cut from American material from New York State. Notable deposits include Agrigento, Sicily (Italy); the area around Bristol (England); Giershagen, Stadtberge (West Germany), Montevecchio Maggiore (Italy); the Katschberg road tunnel, Salzburge, and from the Leogang district of Austria; Machow, Tarnobrzeg (Poland) as slender yellowish crystals. Gem quality crystals are found in geodes in Madagascar. Very large crystals from Kelleys Island, Lake Erie and from Lampasas, Texas (USA); fine blue crystals from Manitou Springs (USA).

Cerussite $PbCO_3$

Aragonite group

Tsumeb, Namibia

Crystal system, form and habit Orthorhombic: varied forms, almost always twinned giving hexagonal shape

Hardness 3-3.5

Cleavage Two directions of distinct prismatic cleavage

Specific gravity 6.55

Colour Colourless; yellow

Lustre Adamantine to vitreous lustre; surface films may look metallic

Refractive index 1.8-2

Streak Colourless to white

Diaphaneity Transparent to translucent

Other features Pale green or blue fluorescence SWUV in some specimens; soluble in, and effervesces with, dilute HNO_3

Name From the Latin name for lead carbonate

Found in the upper oxidized zones of lead ore deposits where it is found with other lead, zinc or copper minerals. Best crystals from Tsumeb (Namibia). Fine crystals from Mies (Czechoslovakia); from the lead deposits at Monteponi, Sardinia (Italy) where it occurs with phosgenite and anglesite; from the Pentire Glaze mine, St Minver, Cornwall (England) and from the Scottish lead mining area around Leadhills, Lanarkshire where it occurs with leadhillite and caledonite;

from the Tynagh mine (Ireland). Cerussite is abundant at North American lead mines, especially from the Wheatley mine, Phoenixville, Pennsylvania; from Broken Hill, New South Wales (Australia); from the Kapi mine (Tasmania); from Guangdong (China). Cerussite has been faceted though its brittleness makes it hard to cut. However, its high lustre and dispersion make it attractive when cutting is successful.

Ceruleite $Cu_2Al_7(AsO_4)_4(OH)_{13}.12H_2O$

Bolivia

Crystal system, form and habit Triclinic, with a density of about 2.80
Colour Deep blue compact clay-like masses resembling turquoise
Name From a word for blue in allusion to its colour

Found in Wheal Gorland, Gwennap, Cornwall (England) and the Emma Luisa gold mine, Huanaco, Taltal (Chile). Some material from Bolivia has been fashioned into cabochons.

Chalcanthite $CuSO_4.5H_2O$

Chalcanthite group

Nevada, USA

Crystal system, form and habit Triclinic, short prismatic crystals; sometimes stalactitic
Hardness 2.5
Cleavage 3 directions, imperfect

Specific gravity 2.28
Colour Sky to deep blue; greenish
Lustre Vitreous
Streak Colourless
Diaphaneity Translucent to transparent
Other features Dehydrates at room temperature to an opaque greenish-white powdery aggregate; this happens most commonly in dry atmospheres. Sweetish metallic taste but poisonous!
Name From the Latin chalcanthum (flowers of copper)

Found with other hydrated sulphates of copper or iron and a feature of arid regions where commercial deposits have been worked. Often a feature of mine workings where it crystallizes from mine water on to timbers and walls. Found at Rammelsberg and Goslar, Harz (West Germany) and as a deposit from fumaroles on Vesuvius (Italy). Found in good crystals at Zajecar, Serbia, (Yugoslavia) and from some Cornish mines, notably the now-closed Tin Tang mine at Gwennap (England). Widespread in the copper mines of California, Colorado and Arizona (USA); good specimens from the Majuba Hill mine, Pershing County, Nevada, (USA), and Guangdong (China).

Chalcocite Cu_2S

Bristol, Connecticut, USA

Crystal system, form and habit Monoclinic, usually massive; some geniculate twinned crystals.
Hardness 2.5-3
Cleavage Poor prismatic
Specific gravity 7.2-7.4
Colour Dark lead grey – may become coated with a brownish black film
Lustre Metallic
Name From its composition

An important source of copper, chalcocite is found with other copper minerals. Fine crystals from sulphide veins in the St Ives Consols mine and the Levant mine, St Just, from Simms lode and North Pig lode, Geevor mine, Cornwall (England); from the Leonard mine area, Butte, Montana (USA); also from Cap Garonne, Var, Garde-en-Oisans, Isere, Framont, Alsace (France).

Chalcopyrite

Chalcopyrite group

$CuFeS_2$

Butte, Montana, USA

Crystal system, form and habit Tetragonal, usually tetrahedral and twinning common
Hardness 3.5-4
Cleavage One poor
Specific gravity 4.1-4.3
Colour Brassy yellow
Lustre Metallic, sometimes tarnished and iridescent
Streak Greenish-black
Other features Soluble in HNO_3
Name From Greek words meaning brass and pyrites

The most common copper mineral, chalcopyrite is an important ore. It occurs in many sulphide deposits though hypothermal and mesothermal vein deposits also show a good deal of the mineral. Fine crystals are found at Freiberg, Saxony (East Germany) and at Siegen, Westphalia (West Germany). Interesting crystals can also be found at Ste Marie aux Mines, Alsace (France). Crystals and botryoidal masses with cassiterite and quartz can be found in the tin veins of Camborne, and from the New Kitty mine, St Agnes, Cornwall (England). Fine crystal groups are found at the Japanese location of Ani and Arakawa, Ugo province. Very large crystals and masses are found at Ellenville, Ulster County, New York (USA). From Kitzbühel, Tirol and Hüttenberg, Carinthia (Austria); Rio Tinto (Spain); Ergani-Maden (Turkey); Camp Bird mine, Ouray County, Colorado (USA); from Campione, Grosseto (Italy) and Jiangxi (China).

Childrenite

$Fe^{2+}Al(PO_4)(OH)_2 \cdot H_2O$

Minas Gerais, Brazil
Crystal system, form and habit Monoclinic, large well formed pink crystals or sheaves of subparallel crystals and radiating sprays. Forms a series with eosphorite which contains more Mn than Fe
Hardness 4.5
Cleavage Good, front and side pinacoid
Specific gravity 3.06-3.25
Colour Salmon-pink, light to dark brown or grey
Lustre Vitreous to pearly
Diaphaneity Translucent to transparent
Name From the English mineralogist J G Children

Both minerals are characteristic of pegmatites and many come from deposits in Minas Gerais (Brazil). Fine sprays of brown crystals with rose quartz at Taquaral (Brazil). Bright brown scattered crystals from deposits in Cornwall and Devon (England), especially from the George and Charlotte mine, Tavistock, Devon and from Crinnis Cliff, St Austell, Cornwall. Also from Hagendorf-Sud, Bavaria (West Germany).

Chondrodite

$(Mg,Fe_{2+})_5(SiO_4)_2(F,OH)_2$

Humite group

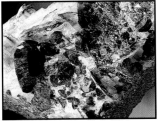

Tilly Foster mine, New York, USA
Crystal system, form and habit Monoclinic, variable habit or massive. Commonly shows lamellar twinning
Hardness 6-6.5
Specific gravity 3.2-3.3
Colour Yellow, red, brown
Lustre Vitreous
Refractive index 1.592-1.646
Diaphaneity Transparent to translucent
Name From the Greek word for grain, alluding to a common habit of the mineral

Found in contact zones in limestone or dolomite. Fine red gem-quality crystals from the Tilly Foster iron mine, Brewster, New York (USA); from Monte Somma (Italy) and from the Pargas area of Finland.

Chromite

Spinel group

$FeCr_2O_4$

Montana, USA

Crystal system, form and habit Cubic, usually massive but some octahedral crystals found
Hardness 5.5
Specific gravity 4.5-4.8
Colour Black
Lustre Metallic
Streak Brown
Name From its composition

Found in igneous rocks rich in olivine, in meteorites and in placer deposits. Many deposits worldwide, in particular Bushveld, Transvaal (South Africa); Kraubath, Styria (Austria); Stillwater, Montana (USA); Fethiye (Turkey). The only ore mineral of chromium.

Chrysoberyl

$BeAl_2O_4$

Lac Alaotra, Madagascar

Crystal system, form and habit Orthorhombic, forming pseudohexagonal twins 'trillings' or found as pebbles
Hardness 8.5
Cleavage 3 minor; parts along twin boundaries
Specific gravity 3.75
Colour Golden, greenish-yellow; dark green, brown
Lustre Vitreous
Refractive index 1.74-1.75
Streak Colourless
Diaphaneity Transparent
Other features Variety alexandrite is green in daylight changing to dark red in tungsten light; cat's-eye shows a sharp white 'eye' against a gold to greenish-brown background; alexandrite may fluoresce red
Name From Greek words meaning golden and beryl

Chrysoberyl is most commonly found alluvially as water-worn pebbles but it can also be found in some granite pegmatites and mica schists. Such deposits are characteristic of the Uralian sources of the Takowaja river, source of fine alexandrite. Alluvial deposits produce alexandrite and cat's-eye from Sri Lanka. Hexagonal aggregates ('trillings') are characteristic of some of the Brazilian deposits and very fine alexandrite with a marked colour change has recently been reported from the area of Hematita, Minas Gerais (Brazil); yellow-green trillings particularly from Itaguaçu, Espirito Santo (Brazil) and also from Orissa (India).

Chrysocolla $(Cu,Al)_2H_2Si_2O_5(OH)_4.nH_2O$

Zacatecas, Mexico

Crystal system, form and habit Monoclinic; usually forms aggregates
Hardness 2.0-2.4, 7 from included quartz

Specific gravity Most ornamental material near 2.6
Colour Blue to blue-green
Lustre Vitreous where silica present; dull
Refractive index 1.57-1.63
Other features May be mixed with copper carbonates or with turquoise. Where mixed with quartz may show its constants. Sectile; tongue may stick to specimen
Name From Greek words meaning golden and glue (from its one-time use in soldering)

Chrysocolla is found in the oxidized zones of copper deposits. When mixed with malachite it can be used ornamentally and may be known as Eilat stone from Eilat in the Gulf of Aqaba, Red Sea. Where little silica is present the mineral is frangible. Blue quartz impregnated by chrysocolla can be found in the Globe mine, Gila County, Arizona (USA); from Cornwall and Cumbria (England) although high-quality specimens not likely to be found today; and from Johnsbach, Steiermark (Austria).

Chrysotile

$Mg_3Si_2O_5(OH)_4$

Kaolinite-serpentine group

Arizona, USA

Crystal system, form and habit Monoclinic; found as fibres
Hardness 2.5
Specific gravity 2.55
Colour White, grey to yellow, green and brown
Lustre Silky to greasy
Refractive index 1.53-1.55
Name From Greek words for gold and fibre alluding to its colour and structure

Found as fibres in serpentine which is a common metamorphic rock with wide distribution. Denser material, sometimes fashioned, from Bernstein, Burgenland (Austria).

Cinnabar

HgS

Hunan, China

Crystal system, form and habit Trigonal, rhombohedral or thick tabular; frequently twinned; usually massive

Hardness 2-2.5
Cleavage One perfect
Specific gravity 8.09
Colour Scarlet red to black or lead grey
Lustre Adamantine to metallic or dull
Refractive index 2.9-3.2
Streak Scarlet to reddish-brown
Diaphaneity Translucent to transparent
Other features Slightly sectile
Name Thought to be of Indian origin

Found in veins in the vicinity of recently formed volcanic rocks, often in association with pyrite, marcasite and stibnite in chalcedony. The chief ore of mercury. Fine crystals from Mount Avala, Belgrade (Yugoslavia) and the most important economic deposit is at Almaden, Ciudad Real (Spain). Other localities include New Almaden, California (USA), Obermoschel and from Grube Silbereckle, Schwarzwald (West Germany); Glatschach (Austria), Monte Amiata, Tuscany (Italy) and from the Styrian Erzberg (Austria). Also from Santa Barbara (Peru), and from the Wan-Shan-Ch'ang mine, Tung-Jen, Yanwuping mine, Wanshan County, Guizhou province (China).

Clinochlore $(MgFe^{2+})_5Al(Si_3Al)O_{10}(OH)_8$

Chlorite group

Tilly Foster mine, Brewster, New York, USA

Crystal system, form and habit Monoclinic, scaly masses of tabular crystals

Hardness 2-2.5
Cleavage 1 perfect micaceous
Specific gravity 2.67
Colour Colourless, pale to deep green
Lustre Pearly, greasy or dull
Refractive index 1.57-1.59
Streak Colourless to greenish-white
Diaphaneity Transparent to opaque
Name From its crystal structure (monoclinic) and from a Greek word for green

Found mostly in schists and metamorphic rocks. Also from the hydrothermal alteration of amphiboles, pyroxenes and biotite in igneous rocks. Localities in the Ala Valley, Piedmont (Italy), Bitsch and Zermatt (Switzerland), Austria, USSR, and Pasadena, California (USA).

Clinoclase $Cu_3(AsO_4)(OH)_3$

St Day, Gwennap, Cornwall, England

Crystal system, form and habit Monoclinic, forming elongated and tabular crystals some

appearing rhombohedral, sometimes grouped into rosettes
Hardness 2.5-3
Cleavage Perfect
Specific gravity 4.33
Colour Dark greenish blue to greenish-black
Lustre Vitreous to pearly
Streak Bluish-green
Diaphaneity Transparent to translucent
Name From its crystal structure and its cleavage

Found as a secondary mineral associated with olivenite. From the Eureka and Mammoth mines, Tintic, Juab County, Utah and at the Gold Hill mine in Tooele County (USA). From Collahuasi, Tarapaca (Chile) and from St Day, Gwennap, Cornwall (England).

Clinohumite

$(Mg,Fe^{2+})_9(SiO_4)_4(F,OH)_2$

Humite group

Italy

Crystal system, form and habit Monoclinic, often twinned
Hardness 6

Cleavage Basal; may be hard to detect
Specific gravity 3.28
Colour Yellow, orange, brown, white
Lustre Vitreous
Refractive index 1.62-1.66
Diaphaneity Transparent to translucent
Other features Some specimens may show yellow fluorescence
Name From its family and crystal structure

Found in serpentines and talc schists or in contact zones in dolomite. Fine transparent orange gem-quality crystals from Lake Baikal, Siberia (USSR). Also from the Tilly Foster iron mine, Brewster, New York (USA); in the Llanos de Junar, Malaga (Spain) and Pargas (Finland).

Clinozoisite

$Ca_2Al_3(SiO_4)_3(OH)$

Epidote group

Eden Mills, Vermont, USA

Crystal system, form and habit Monoclinic, prismatic or tabular, often twinned or massive
Hardness 6.5
Cleavage Perfect basal
Specific gravity 3.21-3.38
Colour Yellow to brown
Lustre Vitreous
Refractive index 1.67-1.73
Streak Greyish
Diaphaneity Transparent to translucent

Other features Strongly pleochroic

Name From the monoclinic form of the crystals

Clinozoisite, the iron-poor member of the epidote group, is dimorphous with zoisite and forming a series with epidote. Finest crystals found at Gavilanes, Baja California (Mexico) and generally characteristic of low- to medium-grade metamorphic rocks and some igneous rocks

Cobaltite CoAsS

Norway and Sweden (cubes)

Crystal system, form and habit Orthorhombic, pseudocubic, cubes and pyritohedra, striated faces; massive
Hardness 5.5
Cleavage Good cubic
Specific gravity 6.32
Colour White or grey with violet tint
Lustre Metallic
Streak Greyish-black
Name From its composition

Found in high temperature hydrothermal vein deposits from Cobalt, Ontario (Canada) and places in California (USA). Fine crystals from Tunaberg, Hakansbö, Riddarhyttan (Sweden); England, USSR, Austria. Also from Annaberg and Schneeberg, Saxony (East Germany); Bou Azzer (Morocco); Montevecchio, Sardinia (Italy).

Colemanite $Ca_2B_6O_{11}.5H_2O$

California, USA
Crystal system, form and

habit Monoclinic, equant, short prismatic, complex terminations or massive
Hardness 4.5
Cleavage 1 perfect side pinacoid
Specific gravity 2.42
Colour Colourless, yellowish
Lustre Vitreous
Diaphaneity Transparent
Name For William Tell Coleman, founder of the American borax industry

Colemanite is found in saline lake deposits, especially from those in Inyo County, California (USA). Fine crystals from Eskisehir (Turkey); also from Inder, Kazakhstan (USSR).

Copper   Cu

Ajo, Arizona, USA
Crystal system, form and habit Cubic; cubes, octahedra, elongated or flattened, twinning

common
Hardness 2.5-3
Specific gravity 8.9
Colour Pale rose tarnishing to copper
Lustre Metallic
Streak Shining pale red
Other features Malleable and ductile
Name From the Latin cuprum, itself derived from the Greek word for Cyprus, early source of the mineral

Found in the oxidized zone of copper bearing sulphide ore deposits; in sedimentary rocks near contacts with basic extrusive rocks or in cavities in basalts and in sandstones. Fine crystals from deposits around the Quincy mine, Hancock, North Michigan and Bisbee, Arizona (USA); Tsumeb (Namibia) and large amounts on the Keweenaw Peninsula. From the New Cornelia mine, Ajo, Arizona (USA) and Jiangxi (China); also England, Scotland, USSR, Siegerland (West Germany).

Cordierite $(Mg,Fe^{3+})_2Al_4Si_5O_{18}$

Richmond, New Hampshire, USA
Crystal system, form and habit Orthorhombic, short

prismatic or massive
Hardness 7-7.5
Cleavage Distinct, side pinacoidal
Specific gravity 2.53-2.78
Colour Blue to violet (pleochroic)
Lustre Vitreous
Refractive index 1.522-1.578
Streak Colourless
Diaphaneity Transparent
Name From the French mining engineer P L A Cordier

Alternatively named iolite, cordierite is found in thermally altered aluminium-rich rocks, gneisses and schists; also from pegmatites and granites. Gem quality material found in Sri Lanka; crystals from Orijarvi (Finland); Otztal, Tirol (Austria); Kragerö (Norway); Haddam, Connecticut (USA).

Cornubite

$Cu_5(AsO_4)_2(OH)_4$

Crystal system, form and habit Triclinic, fibrous or massive
Specific gravity 4.6-4.7
Colour Light to apple-green to dark green
Name From the old Roman name for Cornwall (Cornubia)

Nevada, USA

Found at localities in Cornwall, Devon and Cumbria (England), and Reichenbach, Odenwald (West Germany).

Corundum

Al_2O_3

Hematite group

Sri Lanka
Crystal system, form and habit Trigonal, bipyramids or tabular crystals
Hardness 9

Cleavage Parting prominent
Specific gravity 3.99-4.0
Colour Colourless, red, pink, shades of blue, yellow, green, orange, purple or multicoloured
Lustre Vitreous
Refractive index 1.76-1.77
Diaphaneity Transparent to translucent
Other features Some Fe-free varieties, particularly ruby, fluoresce UV
Name Perhaps from an Indian word kauruntaka, used for the mineral

Corundum includes the gem varieties ruby (red) and sapphire (all other colours). The finest rubies and sapphires are found in the remains of a metamorphosed limestone in Burma and also in Sri Lanka, though the mineral forms under other conditions as well. Almost all gem corundum is recovered from alluvial deposits. Fine examples of ruby also from Pakistan and East Africa; fine ruby and sapphire from Thailand and blue sapphire also from Cambodia, Montana (the Yogo Gulch mine, Utica, USA) and from Australia. Fine yellow sapphire from Australia, Sri Lanka. A pink variety known as padparadschah from Sri Lanka. Non-gem quality material from the Campolungo dolomite, Passo Cadonighino, Ticino (Switzerland). Blue crystals from Emmelberg, Eifel (West Germany); opaque ruby crystals from Fiskenasset (Greenland). Recently reported from Hebei (China).

Covelline CuS

Butte, Montana

Crystal system, form and habit Hexagonal, thin plates, usually massive, foliated

Hardness 1.5-2
Cleavage Perfect basal
Specific gravity 4.68
Colour Light to dark indigo
Lustre Submetallic to dull
Refractive index 1.45
Streak Shining grey-blue
Diaphaneity Translucent in thin pieces
Other features Sectile; purplish iridescence
Name From Niccolo Covelli, Italian mineralogist

Found in the secondary enrichment zone in copper sulphide deposits. Fine crystals in groups from the Leonard mine area, Butte, Montana (USA) and at the Calabona mine, Alghero, Sardinia (Italy); Bor (Yugoslavia); Leogang, Salzburg (Austria).

Creedite

$Ca_3Al_2(SO_4)(F,OH)_{10}.2H_2O$

Potosi mine, Santa Eulalia, Mexico
Crystal system, form and

habit Monoclinic, short prismatic or acicular; clusters or radiated aggregates
Hardness 4
Cleavage Perfect
Specific gravity 2.71
Colour Light purple or colourless
Lustre Vitreous
Refractive index 1.461-1.485
Diaphaneity Transparent
Name From the location

Found in cavities of banded fluorite or as radial masses in granular white barite. Loose doubly-terminated crystals from Wagon Wheel Gap, Creede, Mineral County, Colorado (USA). Fine gem-quality crystals from Santa Eulalia, Chihuahua, (Mexico); fine crystal aggregates from the tin veins of Colquiri (Bolivia)

Crocoite

$PbCrO_4$

Dundas, Tasmania
Crystal system, form and habit Monoclinic, usually pris-

matic, often hollow; striated
Hardness 2.5-3
Cleavage Distinct prismatic
Specific gravity 5.99
Colour Deep orange
Lustre Adamantine to vitreous
Streak Orange-yellow
Diaphaneity Translucent
Other features Crystal faces noticeably smooth
Name From a Greek word alluding to the colour

Though the mines of the Dundas area (Tasmania) provide many fine crystals for collectors, crocoite is also found in the Beresov district, Ural Mountains and from Rezbanya (Romania). Good crystals are reported from Goyabeira, Minas Gerais (Brazil). It is found with wulfenite at the Darwin mines, Inyo County, California and at the Mammoth mine, Pinal County, Arizona (USA) where it occurs with wulfenite and vanadinite. Crocoite is found in the gossan of mineral deposits.

Cumengeite

$Pb_{21}Cu_{20}Cl_{42}(OH)_{40}$

Boleo, Baja California, Mexico

Crystal system, form and habit Tetragonal, octahedral crystals or overgrowths on boleite or pseudoboleite giving at twinned appearance
Hardness 2.5
Cleavage Good
Specific gravity 4.6
Colour Indigo
Lustre Vitreous
Streak Sky blue
Diaphaneity Translucent
Name From Edouard Cumenge, French mining engineer

Found as a secondary mineral with boleite at Boleo, Baja California (Mexico)

Cuprite

Cu_2O

Copper Queen mine, Bisbee, Arizona, USA

Crystal system, form and habit Cubic, octahedral
Hardness 3.5-4
Cleavage Poor octahedral
Specific gravity 6.14
Colour Red
Lustre Adamantine or metallic
Refractive index 2.84
Streak Brownish-red
Diaphaneity Translucent, transparent
Other features Soluble in HCl
Name From a Greek word for copper

Found in the oxidized zone of copper deposits and associated with malachite and other copper minerals. Very fine clear crystals from the Onganja mine (Namibia). Some of these have been faceted though they tend to develop a surface coating on exposure to light – the coating can be removed by polishing. Very fine crystals also from Bisbee, Arizona (USA). Fine specimens from Redruth and Liskeard in Cornwall (England). The variety chalcotrichite, which produces hair-like crystals, is also found in Cornwall, particularly from the Fowey Consols mine, St Blazey. Brilliant larger red crystals from the Phoenix mine, Linkinhorne. In Europe chalcotrichite is found at Leogang,

Salzburg (Austria) and Rheinbreitbach (West Germany). Good crystals from Chessy (France) and from the USSR.

Danburite $CaB(SiO_4)_2$

Charcas, Mexico
Crystal system, form and habit Orthorhombic, prismatic, diamond shaped cross section

Hardness 7
Cleavage Poor basal
Specific gravity 3.00
Colour Colourless to yellowish-brown
Lustre Vitreous to greasy
Refractive index 1.63-1.64
Streak Colourless
Diaphaneity Transparent to translucent
Other features Fluoresces sky-blue
Name From the locality at Danbury, Connecticut (USA)

Found in the pegmatites of Mt Bity (Madagascar); fine crystals from Charcas, San Luis Potosi (Mexico); fine crystals with axinite at the Toroku mine, Miyazake (Japan); with ruby in dolomitic marble in Mogok (Burma); in a fissure at Skopi (Switzerland).

Datolite $CaBSiO_4(OH)$

Gadolinite group

New Jersey, USA
Crystal system, form and habit Monoclinic, short

prismatic
Hardness 5-5.5
Specific gravity 3
Colour Colourless, pale yellow
Lustre Vitreous
Refractive index 1.62-1.70
Streak Colourless
Diaphaneity Transparent to translucent
Name From a Greek word meaning to divide, alluding to the granular nature of some datolite

Datolite is found as a secondary mineral in basic igneous rocks and is associated with zeolites and calcite It also occurs in crevices in granite. Fine large crystals at the Lane quarry, West-field, Massachusetts (USA) and in the trap rocks of northern New Jersey (USA). Also from England, Norway, Czechoslo-vakia, USSR. Large greenish crystals from the danburite occur-rence at Charcas (Mexico).

Descloizite

$PbZn(VO_4)(OH)$

Descloizite group

Grootfontein, Namibia

aggregates
Hardness 3-3.5
Specific gravity 6.26
Colour Orange to dark reddish-brown or green
Lustre Vitreous to greasy
Refractive index 2.18-2.35
Streak Yellowish-orange to brownish-red
Diaphaneity Transparent to translucent
Name From the French mineral-ogist L E G Des Cloizeaux

Crystal system, form and habit Orthorhombic, usually pyramidal, prismatic, tabular;

Descloizite is a secondary mineral in the oxidation zone of ore deposits. Superb crystal groups from Tsumeb (Namibia); Silver Queen mine, Galena, South Dakota (USA); Obir, Carinthia (Austria); Liaoning (China). Forms a series with mottramite.

Diamond

C

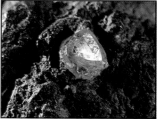

South Africa

Hardness 10
Cleavage Perfect octahedral
Specific gravity 3.52
Colour Colourless, yellow, green, blue, pink
Lustre Adamantine
Refractive index 2.42
Diaphaneity Transparent
Other features May fluoresce in LWUV; blue fluorescence with yellow phosphorescence diagnostic.
Name From the Greek word adamas, meaning indestructibility

Crystal system, form and habit Cubic, octahedra, cubes, dodecahedra, often flattened and twinned.

Found mainly in 'pipes' of a serpentinized olivine known as kimberlite; also alluvially. Associated in the kimberlite with pyrope, olivine, enstatite and phlogopite. Some diamonds (lonsdaleite) found in meteorites. Main sources for commercial diamonds are the western, central and southern countries of Africa; also from Siberia, Venezuela; from isolated locations in the USA, India and Australia; reported from China (Hunan, Jiangsu, Liasning and Shandong). Dimorphous with graphite.

Diaspore AlO(OH)

Massachusetts, USA

Crystal system, form and habit Orthorhombic, forming elongated platy crystals and some thicker ones, some of which have been faceted

Hardness 6.5-7
Cleavage Perfect
Specific gravity 3.3-3.5
Colour Pale yellow but some specimens may show colour change to pinkish-brown in incandescent light
Lustre Vitreous
Refractive index 1.702-1.750
Name From the Greek word to scatter, referring to the mineral's easy disintegration in the blow-pipe flame

Large crystals from a vein in aluminium-rich rocks at Mamaris, Yatagan, Mugla (Turkey).

Diopside $CaMgSi_2O_6$
Pyroxene group

Kunlun Mountains, China

Crystal system, form and

habit Monoclinic, stubby crystals
Hardness 5.5-6.5
Cleavage Perfect prismatic
Specific gravity 3.22-3.38
Colour Various responses to UV. Dark to light, sometimes emerald-green, brown.
Lustre Vitreous
Refractive index 1.664-1.721
Diaphaneity Translucent to transparent
Other features Four-rayed star

and chatoyant stones are known. Some light-coloured crystals from dolomitic marble may fluoresce blue

Name From two Greek words meaning double appearance

Found in calcium-rich metamorphic rocks and in kimberlites with diamond. Fine green specimens from Outukumpu (Finland), Ural Mountains (USSR), Kimberley (South Africa); yellow and violet varieties from the gem areas of Burma; green crystals from the Zillertal (Austria) and from De Kalb, New York (USA); fine green crystals from Val d'Ossola, Novara (Italy). Forms a series with hedenbergite.

Dioptase

$CuSiO_2(OH)_2$

Namibia

Crystal system, form and habit Trigonal, forming attractive crystal groups of stubby individuals.

Hardness 5
Cleavage Perfect rhombohedral
Specific gravity 3.28-3.35
Colour Dark emerald-green
Lustre Vitreous
Refractive index 1.644-1.709
Diaphaneity Transparent to translucent
Other features High dispersion
Name From the Greek with reference to the ease of seeing the cleavage direction through the crystal

Found in the oxidized zone of copper deposits, especially from Katanga (Zaire). Also occurs in the Tsumeb area of Namibia, particularly the Omaue mine, Kaoko-Veld; the Altyn-Tube area of the Khirgiz Steppes (USSR); Copiapo (Chile).

Dolomite

$CaMg(CO_3)_2$

Pyroxene group

Bou Azzer, Morocco

Crystal system, form and habit Trigonal, rhombohedrons

with curved faces; masses
Hardness 3.5-4
Cleavage Perfect rhombohedral
Specific gravity 2.85
Colour Colourless, pink, pale brown
Lustre Vitreous to pearly
Refractive index 1.50-1.67
Diaphaneity Transparent to translucent
Name From French geologist D G S T Gratet de Dolomieu

Widespread occurrence. Fine crystals from Egui, Navarra (Spain); the Missouri-Oklahoma-Kansas lead-zinc deposits (USA): the Lockport dolomite, New York (USA) and from St Eustache, Quebec (Canada). Some of the Spanish crystals have been faceted. Also from the Binntal (Switzerland); Leogang, Salzburg (Austria); Traversella, Piedmont (Italy); Rézbánya (Hungary).

Dravite

$NaMg_3Al_6(BO_3)_3Si_6O_{18}(OH,F)_4$

Tourmaline group

Western Australia

Crystal system, form and habit Trigonal, forming striated

prismatic crystals
Hardness 7.25
Specific gravity 3.03-3.15
Colour Usually brown to black
Lustre Vitreous
Refractive index 1.62-1.64 (constants vary widely through chemical substitution)
Streak Colourless
Diaphaneity Transparent
Name From Drave, Carinthia (Austria)

Found in metamorphic and metasomatic rocks, and pegmatites. Fine crystals from Gouverneur, St Lawrence County, New York (USA); very fine crystals with pyramid form from Yinnietharra, (Australia); Crevoladossola, Novara (Italy). Forms series with elbaite and with schorl.

Dufrenite

$$Fe^{2+}Fe_4^{3+}(PO_4)_3(OH)_5.2H_2O$$

Auerbach, West Germany

Crystal system, form and habit Monoclinic; crusts or masses often botryoidal
Hardness 3.5-4.5

Cleavage Perfect side and front pinacoid
Specific gravity 3.1-3.3
Colour Dark green to greenish-black
Lustre Vitreous to silky
Refractive index 1.82-1.95
Streak Yellow-green
Diaphaneity Translucent
Other features Becomes greenish-brown to reddish brown from oxidation
Name From French mineralogist O P A P Dufrenoy

Usually occurs as a green film on minerals in iron mines or pegmatites. Found at Wheal Phoenix, Redruth, Cornwall (England); deposits in Germany, especially at Hagendorf, Bavaria.

Dumortierite

$$Al_7(BO_3)(SiO_4)_3O_3$$

Nevada, USA

Crystal system, form and habit Orthorhombic, prismatic;

usually massive, fibrous
Hardness 7
Cleavage Poor pinacoidal
Specific gravity 3.26-3.41
Colour Blue to greenish, pink or violet
Lustre Vitreous to dull
Refractive index 1.68-1.72
Diaphaneity Translucent
Other features Some material gives blue fluorescence SWUV
Name For Eugene Dumortier, paleontologist

Massive dumortierite in blue and violet is used ornamentally – crystals are rare. It occurs in aluminous metamorphic rocks. Some Brazilian (Minas Gerais) material is transparent enough to facet. Gem material may also be found in Arizona (USA).

Has been used to imitate lapis lazuli. Purple fluorescing material from San Diego county, California (USA).

Durangite

NaAl(AsO$_4$)F

Thomas Range, Utah, USA

Crystal system, form and habit Monoclinic oblique pyramidal crystals with rough or dull faces
Hardness 5
Cleavage Distinct
Specific gravity 3.9
Colour Light to dark orange-red
Lustre Vitreous
Streak Yellowish
Diaphaneity Translucent
Name From the location

Found with cassiterite, topaz and hematite at the Barranca tin mine, Durango (Mexico)

Elbaite

Na(Li,Al)$_3$Al$_6$(BO$_3$)$_3$Si$_6$O$_{18}$(OH)$_4$

Tourmaline group

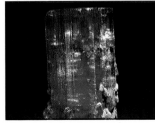

Minas Gerais, Brazil
Crystal system, form and habit Trigonal, forming series to dravite. Prismatic crystals, deeply

striated
Hardness 7.25
Specific gravity 3.03-3.1
Colour Shades of green, red, colourless, blue, yellow or multi-coloured
Lustre Vitreous
Refractive index 1.62-1.64 – constants vary due to complex chemical substitutions
Streak Colourless
Diaphaneity Transparent
Name From the Island of Elba

Tourmalines are particularly associated with pegmatites. Fine elbaite crystals are found in many locations in Minas Gerais (Brazil); San Diego County, California, and Maine (USA); also from the Urals (USSR), Namibia, Madagascar; Grotta d'Oggi, Elba (Italy); Laghman (Afghanistan); Pakistan. Bright grass-green, yellow to amber manganese-rich crystals, also pink, lemon-yellow and green tricoloured and 'water-melon' (green rind, pink core) crystals from pegmatites in the Sankhuwa Sabha district, Kosi zone (Nepal). Also from Xinjiang Uygur (China).

Enstatite

$MgSi_2O_6$

Pyroxene group

Voxnös, Arendal, Norway

Crystal system, form and habit Orthorhombic, crystals prismatic, often showing lamellar

twinning
Hardness 5-6
Cleavage Perfect prismatic
Specific gravity 3.2-3.3
Colour Green, emerald-green to brown
Lustre Vitreous
Refractive index 1.650-1.680
Streak Pink to green pleochroism
Diaphaneity Transparent to translucent
Name From Greek words alluding to its high melting point

Found in basic and ultrabasic rocks and other environments. Chrome (emerald) green stones have been found with diamond at Kimberley (South Africa); green and brown stones used as gems usually come from India or Brazil. Some specimens show four or six-rayed stars. Enstatite forms a series with iron silicates, hypersthene, bronzite and orthoferrosilite.

Eosphorite

$MnAl(PO_4)(OH)_2.H_2O$

Conselheiro Pena, Minas Gerais, Brazil

Crystal system, form and habit Monoclinic forming short

to long prismatic crystals, often twinned; also radiating aggregates
Hardness 5
Specific gravity 3.05
Colour Colourless to pale pink to reddish-brown
Lustre Vitreous to resinous
Refractive index 1.638-1.671
Diaphaneity Transparent to translucent
Name From a Greek word alluding to dawn, with reference to the colour

Forms a series with childrenite and found in granite pegmatites. Fine specimens from Minas Gerais (Brazil) and Hagendorf, Bavaria (West Germany).

Epidote

$Ca_2(Al,Fe^{3+})_3(SiO_4)_3(OH)$

Epidote group

Austria

Crystal system, form and habit Monoclinic, prismatic or tabular, often twinned or massive
Hardness 6-7

Cleavage Perfect basal
Specific gravity 3.38-3.49
Colour Green to brown
Lustre Vitreous
Refractive index 1.715-1.797
Diaphaneity Transparent to translucent
Other features Strongly pleochroic
Name From a Greek word meaning to increase, with reference to the base of the prism which has one side longer than the other

Found in low- to medium-grade metamorphic rocks and some igneous rocks. Fine crystals from the Green Monster deposit, Prince of Wales Island (Alaska) and the Julie claim, Mineral County, Nevada (USA). Characteristic of many Alpine locations: Knappenwand, Untersulzbachtal, and the Hohe Tauern (Austria); the Gotthard and Tavetsch areas, and fine yellow and pink mixed crystals of epidote, clinozoisite, and piemontite from Poncione Alzasca, Ticino (Switzerland). Recently reported from from Hebei (China). Tawmawite is an emerald green rock from Burma, unakite a rock composed of greenish epidote with pink feldspar from Zimbabwe and parts of southern USA.

Epistilbite

$CaAl_2Si_6O_{16}.5H_2O$

Zeolite group

Teigarhorn, Iceland

Crystal system, form and habit Monoclinic, prismatic, twinned in radial spherical aggregates
Hardness 4
Cleavage Perfect
Specific gravity 2.25
Colour Colourless, pinkish
Lustre Vitreous
Refractive index 1.485-1.519
Name From a Greek word meaning near and stilbite

Found in traprocks at Bergen Hill, New Jersey, (USA); Isle of Skye (Scotland); Poona (India); Val d'Ossola, Novara (Italy).

Epsomite

$MgSO_4.7H_2O$

Douglas County, Oregon, USA
Crystal system, form and habit Orthorhombic, usually as

crusts, masses or efflorescences
Hardness 2-2.5
Cleavage Perfect
Specific gravity 1.67
Colour Colourless or pinkish, greenish
Lustre Usually silky or earthy
Diaphaneity Translucent
Other features Very soluble in water and effloresces in dry air. Saline or bitter taste
Name From location, Epsom (England)

Found as an efflorescence on mine workings and in limestone caverns. From the waters of salt lakes and as fumarolic deposits. From Vesuvius (Italy); Epsom, Surrey (England); Douglas County, Oregon (USA).

Erythrite

$Co_3(AsO_4)_2.8H_2O$

Bou Azzer, Morocco

Hardness 1.5-2.5
Cleavage Perfect micaceous
Specific gravity 3.18
Colour Deep purple to pale pink
Lustre Adamantine to pearly
Refractive index 1.622-1.701
Streak Paler than colour
Diaphaneity Transparent to translucent
Other features Flexible and sectile
Name From a Greek word for red

Crystal system, form and habit Monoclinic, prismatic, flattened or bladed aggregates

Found as a secondary mineral in the oxidized zones of cobalt ore deposits and forms a series with annabergite. Forms as a surface alteration of primary cobalt arsenides. Fine radiating bladed crystals in quartz from Schneeberg, Saxony (East Germany). Also from Richelsdorf, Hesse (West Germany). Bright needle-like crystals found at the Pednandrea mine, Redruth, Cornwall (England). From the Nipissing mine, Cobalt, Ontario (Canada) and fine crystals from Bou Azzer, Anti Atlas (Morocco), and Talmesi (Iran). From Valensuela's mine, Aquiles Serdan, Chihuahua (Mexico). Erythrite has been called 'cobalt bloom'.

Euclase

$BeAlSiO_4(OH)$

Brazil

Crystal system, form and habit Monoclinic, tabular or prismatic
Hardness 6.5-7.5
Cleavage Perfect
Specific gravity 2.99-3.10
Colour Colourless, pale blue, yellow, pale green
Lustre Vitreous
Refractive index 1.650-1.676
Diaphaneity Transparent
Name From its cleavage

Euclase is found in granite pegmatites in such places as Dom Bosco, Ouro Preto, Minas Gerais (Brazil) where it is associated with topaz. Also from the Sanarka River (USSR). Dark blue crystals from the emerald deposits in Colombia and from Zimbabwe. From the Windtal, South Tirol (Austria). Despite the cleavage some transparent specimens are faceted for collectors.

Eudialyte $Na_4(Ca,Ce)_2(Fe^{2+},Mn,Y)ZrSi_8O_{22}(OH,C$

Magnet Cove, Arkansas, USA
Crystal system, form and

habit Trigonal, thick or thin tabular, rhombohedral
Hardness 5-6
Cleavage Indistinct, basal
Specific gravity 2.74-2.98
Colour Yellowish-brown, pink to red
Lustre Vitreous to dull
Refractive index 1.591-1.633
Diaphaneity Translucent
Name From Greek words referring to its easy solubility in acids

Occurs in nepheline syenites and their pegmatites. Fine crystals from Julianehaab (Greenland); Carlingford (Ireland): Langesundfjord (Norway); Kola Peninsula (USSR); Madagascar; Mont St Hilaire, Quebec (Canada).

Feldspars

There are two groups of feldspars, potassium and plagioclase. Potassium feldspars ($KAlSi_3O_8$) have different structures: orthoclase, sanidine and anorthoclase are monoclinic, while microcline is trilinic. The plagioclases have a solid solution between albite ($NaASi_3O_8$) and anorthite ($CaAl_2Si_2O_8$) and are usually divided into six species: albite, oligoclase, andesine, labradorite, bytownite and anorthite.

Crystal system, form and habit Orthoclase: occurs in fine large crystals with rounded faces. Sanidine/anorthoclase: monoclinic, occurring as glassy lumps. Albite: forms triclinic twinned platy crystals in pegmatites and granites. Microcline: is triclinic and occurs as well formed crystals which are often twinned, with the two directions of cleavage common to the orthoclase group

Hardness Orthoclase: 6-6.5; sanidine: 6; albite: 6-6.5; microcline: 6-6.5
Cleavage Orthoclase: perfect
Specific gravity Orthoclase: 2.55-2.63; sanidine: 2.52-2.62; albite 2.63; oligoclase: 2.57; microcline: 2.54-2.63
Colour Orthoclase: yellow, some green material reported; Albite: crystals are white, yellow, pink, green, grey and reddish

Lustre Orthoclase: vitreous
Refractive index Orthoclase:
1.518-1.539; sanidine: 1.518-
1.534; albite: 1.535-1.544; oligoclase: 1.52-1.527; microcline:
1.514-1.539
Diaphaneity Transparent
Other features Orthoclase:
weak blue fluorescence LWUV,
orange SWUV, white to violet
under x-rays; sanidine: resembles
smoky quartz when cut; albite:
moonstone is quite common;
microcline: may show yellow-
green fluorescence LWUV
Name Feldspar named from
Swedish words for field and spar,
referring to the spar in fields lying
on granite. Orthoclase refers to
the cleavage angle of 90°; sanidine from a Greek word for tablet
in allusion to its habit; albite from
its white colour; anorthite from
Greek for 'not straight' and 'fracture' in allusion to its triclinic
symmetry: labradorite from
Labrador; oligoclase from Greek
words meaning 'little fracture'

Anorthite: Mount Vesuvius, Italy

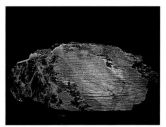
Labradorite: Sweden

Microcline: Lake George, Colorado, USA

Oligoclase: North Carolina, USA

Orthoclase: Baveno, Italy

Sanidine: San Carlos, Arizona, USA

Orthoclase is found in granites, pegmatites, alkalic and plutonic acid rocks; fine crystals from pegmatites at Itrongahy, Madagascar; a sodium-bearing variety (adularia) found in Switzerland. Orange orthoclase sunstone from Tvedestrand (Norway). Yellow and colourless chatoyant stones from Burma and Sri Lanka. Moonstone is orthoclase with lamellar albite inclusions giving the characteristic glow.

Sanidine is found in acid igneous rocks, mostly from the Eifel region of West Germany.

Albite is a fine colourless material from many places, for example the Rutherford pegmatite, Amelia, Virginia (USA). This is the variety known as cleavelandite.

Oligoclase has been found as colourless to pale green transparent crystals at the Hawk mine, Bakersville, North Carolina (USA). Both oligoclase and labradorite may contain included hematite or goethite which give a red to golden colour, the material then being called sunstone. The best material comes from Tvedestrand and Hittero (Norway) and attractive material from the Harts Range, Northern Territory (Australia).

Microcline is found in acid plutonic rocks or in pegmatites, granites and schists. Fine greenish-blue crystals with whitish streaks from Amelia, Virginia, Pike's Peak and Crystal Peak, Colorado (USA). Also USSR and Brazil.

Labradorite is colourless to yellow transparent but some specimens show a play of other colours from inclusions; fine specimens show a schiller (interference effect) of blue, green and gold against an opaque or translucent background. This arises from the presence of another feldspar variety in the labradorite. Best material from the Larvik area of Norway.

Fluorapatite

$Ca_5(PO_4)_3F$

Apatite group

Panasqueira, Portugal

Crystal system, form and habit Hexagonal, prismatic crystals, pyramidal terminations

Hardness 5

Cleavage Indistinct basal and prismatic

Specific gravity 3.10-3.35

Colour Yellow-green, blue, mauve, purple

Lustre Vitreous

Refractive index 1.632-1.642

Diaphaneity Transparent

Other features Rare earth absorption spectrum often clearly seen in yellow specimens. Variable but on the whole undiagnostic luminescence

Name From a Greek word meaning to deceive, referring to the early confusion of apatite with other minerals

Found most commonly in pegmatites. Fine yellow crystals from Durango (Mexico) and violet crystals from Ehrenfriesdorf, Saxony (East Germany). From Emmelberg, Eifel (West Germany) and purple crystals formerly from Greifenstein, Geyer (East Germany). Yellow hexagonal platy crystals from Panasqueira (Portugal). Doubly-terminated blue-green formerly from Luxulyan, and from Rinsey-Tremearne, Cornwall (England); also from the Bovey Tracey area of Devon (England). From Tavetsch (Switzerland) and from Anhui (China). Fine violet crystals from the Pulsifer quarry, Androscoggin County, Maine (USA). Fine blue crystals from Brazil, Burma and Sri Lanka. Some material from Brazil is greenish and chatoyant.

Fluorite

CaF_2

Fort Wayne, Indiana, USA

Crystal system, form and habit Cubic: cubes and interpenetrant twins

Hardness 4

Cleavage Perfect octahedral

Specific gravity 3.18

Colour Greens and blues predominate: yellow and pink also found: bicolour: banded violet and white

Lustre Vitreous: pearly on cleavage surfaces

Refractive index 1.43

Diaphaneity Transparent
Other features Fluoresces blue or violet LWUV. Blue John inert.

Colour from colour centres
Name From its use as a flux from the Latin fluere (to flow)

Found in veins with lead and silver ores or in pneumatolytic deposits with cassiterite, topaz and quartz or in cavities in sedimentary rocks with celestine and barite. Also found as a member of the Alpine 'Kluftmineralien' in joints in granite and other igneous rocks. Fine green, blue and purple crystals with rarer yellows occur in the Northern Pennine orefield of north-east England: Blue John, the chevron-banded violet and white translucent material only from Derbyshire (England). Also from England come green and other coloured crystals from areas in Cornwall, notably the Trevaunance mine, St Agnes, Carn Brea, Redruth and Colcerrow quarry, Luxulyan. Pink crystals from the Aar massif and from the Zinggenstock (Switzerland), the latter location providing some rose-coloured material. Some of the crystals from Switzerland are found as octahedral – a rare occurrence for fluorite. Found at the Silius mine, Sardinia and rare 'scalenohedral' crystals from Wolsendorf, Bavaria (West Germany). Purple and golden crystals from Ehrenfriedsdorf, Saxony (East Germany) and from the Gioia quarry, Carrara marble producing area of Italy. Fine emerald-green crystals from Namibia and from Westmoreland, New Hampshire (USA), where it occurs in veins in gneiss. Spectacular cubes with light yellow bodies and a purple edging from the mining area straddling Illinois and western Kentucky, notably from the Rosiclare district and from Cave-in-Rock, Hardin County, Illinois (USA). Fine coloured crystals from Mont St Hilaire, Quebec (Canada). Fluorite is reported from some locations in China, particularly from Hunan and Anhui.

Friedelite

$Mn_8Si_6O_{15}(OH,CL)_{10}$

New Jersey, USA
Crystal system, form and

habit Monoclinic, pseudotrigonal, tabular, acicular crystals, usually found as masses
Hardness 4-5
Cleavage One perfect
Specific gravity 3.04-3.07
Colour Pale pink to dark brownish-red
Lustre Vitreous
Refractive index 1.62-1.66
Name From Charles Friedel, French mineralogist

Friedelite is found in manganese deposits and most ornamental material is from Franklin, New Jersey (USA). Also found at Adervielle (France) and Orebro (Sweden).

Galena

PbS

Iron Cap mine, Arizona, USA
Crystal system, form and

habit Cubic; cubes, octahedra often twinned or massive
Hardness 2.5-2.75
Cleavage Perfect cubic
Specific gravity 7.58
Colour Lead grey
Lustre 3.91
Streak Lead grey
Diaphaneity Opaque
Name From the Latin word meaning dross that remains after melting lead

Found in limestones, dolomites or in hydrothermal ore veins and contact metamorphic deposits. Worldwide occurrence but notable specimens from Clausthal and St Andreasberg, Harz (West Germany); the northern and southern limestone Alps, Trepca (Yugoslavia); Iglesias, Sardinia (Italy). From Leadhills (Scotland); Herodsfoot mine, Lanreath and Wheal Hope, Perranzabuloe, Cornwall (England); from Galena and the Joplin district of Missouri (USA).

Glauberite

$Na_2Ca(SO_4)_2$

Searles Lake, California, USA
Crystal system, form and

habit Monoclinic, forming steeply bipyramidal crystals
Hardness 2.5-3
Cleavage Perfect basal
Specific gravity 2.7-2.8
Colour White or light yellow to grey
Other features May phosphoresce. Bitter taste. Partially soluble in water in which it whitens.
Name From the German chemist J R Glauber

Found in dry salt lake beds in desert regions. Stassfurt (East Germany); Searles Lake, California (USA); trap rocks of New

Jersey (USA) show quartz casts after glauberite. Opal 'pineapples' may be pseudomorphs after glauberite.

Glaucophane $Na_2(Mg,Fe^{2+})_3Al_2Si_8O_{22}(OH)_2$

Amphibole group

Colorado, USA
Crystal system, form and habit Monoclinic, slender prismatic; sometimes twinned; usually massive
Hardness 6
Cleavage Perfect
Specific gravity 3.1
Colour Grey to bluish-black or lavender
Lustre Vitreous to dull or pearly
Refractive index 1.606-1.670
Streak Greyish-blue
Name From Greek words signifying its colour

Found in crystalline schists, especially in the Coast Ranges of California and at Iron Hill, Gunnison County, Colorado (USA). Also from Scotland, Switzerland and Italy.

Goethite α-$Fe^{+3}O(OH)$

Lake George, Colorado, USA
Crystal system, form and habit Orthorhombic, prismatic or thin tablets; tufts, radiating clusters commonly as masses
Hardness 5-5.5
Cleavage Perfect side pinacoidal
Specific gravity 3.3-4.3
Colour Blackish-brown; yellow or reddish-brown
Lustre Adamantine to dull
Streak Orange to brownish-yellow
Diaphaneity Translucent in thin splinters
Name For Johann Wolfgang von Goethe, German philosopher and poet

Found in many places as an alteration product of iron-bearing minerals such as pyrite and siderite. The most important ore of iron after hematite. Fine radiating terminated crystal clusters from pegmatite pockets at Florissant, Colorado (USA); from the Restormel mine, Lanlivery, Cornwall (England).

Gold

Au

Grass Valley, California, USA

Crystal system, form and habit Cubic; octahedral, dodeca-hedral or cubic crystals; twinning common; arborescent or as grains
Hardness 2.5-3
Specific gravity 19.29
Colour Golden yellow to white or orange-red
Lustre Metallic
Streak Same as colour
Other features Highly ductile and malleable
Name From an Old English word for the metal

Forms a series with silver and found usually in hydrothermal veins with pyrite and other sulphides and in placer deposits. Widespread throughout the Earth. Notable material from hydrothermal vein deposits in the Mother Lode, California and from volcanic rocks at Cripple Creek, Colorado and the Comstock Lode, Nevada (USA). Other hydrothermal vein deposits include the Black Hills, South Dakota (USA); Mysore (India); Hohe Tauern and the Zillertal, Tirol (Austria) and the Fichtelgebirge (West Germany). Also from Beresovsk, Urals (USSR). Other volcanic rock occurrences include the celebrated Romanian deposits at Nagyag and Verespatak. Placer deposits include the Klondike, Yukon, (Canada); Aldan, Siberia (USSR); Witwatersrand (South Africa). Minor locations occur in Wales and from Hope's Nose, Torquay, Devon (England). Reported from Heilongjiang and Guangxi (China).

Grandidierite

$(Mg,Fe^{2+})Al_3(BO_4)(SiO_4)O$

Madagascar

Crystal system, form and habit Orthorhombic, elongated or masses
Hardness 7.5
Cleavage 1 perfect
Specific gravity 2.97
Colour Greenish blue
Lustre Vitreous
Refractive index 1.590-1.639
Name From the French explorer Alfred Grandidier

Found in some pegmatites in Madagascar and sometimes used ornamentally.

Graphite

C

Colombo, Ceylon
Crystal system, form and habit Hexagonal, fine foliated

masses
Hardness 1-2
Cleavage Perfect basal
Specific gravity 2.1
Colour Iron black to steel grey
Lustre Metallic or dull
Diaphaneity Opaque
Other features Flexible and sectile; greasy feel; stains fingers
Name From the Greek word meaning to write, alluding to its use in pencils

Usually found in strongly metamorphosed rocks in many places in the world. Dimorphous with diamond and lonsdaleite. Large deposits at Pargas (Finland); Kropfmühl, Bavaria (West Germany); Ticonderoga, New York (USA).

Greenockite

CdS

Bishopton, Scotland

Crystal system, form and habit Hexagonal, hemimorphic bipyramidal

Hardness 3-3.5
Cleavage Distinct prismatic, poor basal
Specific gravity 4.9
Colour Yellow-orange
Lustre Adamantine to resinous
Refractive index 2.52-2.50
Streak Orange-yellow to brick red
Diaphaneity Transparent to translucent
Name From Lord Greenock

Greenockite is found as a coating on some zinc minerals, particularly sphalerite. At Bishopton, Renfrew (Scotland) crystals occur in the cavities of a labradorite porphyry on prehnite with natrolite and calcite. This is the most important world location. Synthetic greenockite is sometimes faceted. Orange-red minute crystals from Llallagua (Bolivia) found with pyrite.

Grossular

$Ca_3Al_2(SiO_4)_3$

Garnet group

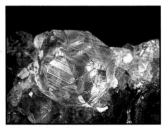

Asbestos, Canada

Crystal system, form and habit Cubic, forming rhombic dodecahedra, icositetrahedra or combinations.

Hardness 6.5-7
Specific gravity 3.4-3.6
Colour Colourless, green, yellowish-green, pink, brown, orange
Lustre Vitreous to resinous
Refractive index 1.734-1.75
Streak White
Name From the Latin word for gooseberry in allusion to the colour of some specimens

Found chiefly in metamorphosed impure calcareous rocks, especially in contact zones. Many colour varieties have gem application and some have their own names. They include hydrogrossular, translucent green (South Africa), tsavolite, bluish to emerald-green, from the Lualenyi mine, Voi (Kenya), from Pakistan and Tanzania, and hessonite, cinnamon colour, from Sri Lanka and Brazil; also as fine crystals from Eden Mills, Vermont (USA). Forms series with andradite and with uvarovite. Hessonite from Pizzo dei Rossi, Ticino (Switzerland); Koutalas, Serifos (Greece).

Gummite

New Hampshire, USA

Crystal system, form and habit Name given to uranium

oxides perhaps containing water
Hardness 2.5-5
Specific gravity 3.9-6.4
Colour Orange-red to greyish-yellow
Other features A mixture of several uranium oxides, silicates and salts, always pseudomorphous after uraninite
Name From gum in allusion to the appearance of some specimens

Forms dendritic growth in feldspars. Brilliant red-orange material found in Rajasthan and Ajmer (India); Czechoslovakia and Saxony (East Germany). Large dendrites at the Ruggles mine, Grafton County, New Hampshire (USA).

Gypsum $CaSO_4.2H_2O$

Mexico

Crystal system, form and habit Monoclinic; thin to thick tabular; swallow-tailed twins

Hardness 2
Cleavage 2 directions, 1 perfect, micaceous
Specific gravity 2.32
Colour Colourless, yellowish, greenish or brownish
Lustre Pearly
Refractive index 1.520-1.529
Streak White
Other features Greenish-white or yellow fluorescence and phosphorescence. Sectile
Name From the Greek word for plaster

Found widespread and chiefly in sedimentary deposits and in saline lakes; in the oxidized zones of ore deposits and volcanic deposits. Rock-forming gypsum from the Bellerophon strata of the Dolomites. Glassy crystals found loose and whole in clay beds are known as selenite and are found at Eisleben, Harz (West Germany); Gypsum 'roses' from El Golea, Sahara (Algeria).

Halite

NaCl

Austria

Crystal system, form and habit Cubic; cubes, sometimes octahedra; hopper crystals; massive or stalactitic
Hardness 2.5
Cleavage Perfect cubic
Specific gravity 2.16
Colour Colourless, orange, purple or blue
Lustre Vitreous
Refractive index 1.544
Other features Soluble in water; some red fluorescence from impurities
Name From the Greek word for salt

Found in sedimentary deposits, some of great size. Also as an efflorescence on mine equipment and walls. From Wieliczka (Poland); Stassfurt (West Germany); Hallstein (Austria); Lungro (Italy); Xinjiang and Qinghai (China).

Hambergite

Be$_2$BO$_3$(OH)

Imalo, Madagascar

Crystal system, form and habit Orthorhombic, flattened prismatic, sometimes twinned
Hardness 7.5
Cleavage Perfect
Specific gravity 2.37
Colour Colourless to yellowish or grey
Lustre Vitreous to dull
Refractive index 1.55-1.63
Name From the Swedish mineralogist Axel Hamberg

Found in alkali-rich pegmatites in Madagascar, particularly at Anjanabanoana; gem gravels in Kashmir and in syenite pegmatite at Langesundfjord (Norway).

Harmotome

$(Ba,K)_{1-2}(Si,Al)_8O_{16}.6H_2O$

Strontian, Argyll, Scotland

Crystal system, form and habit Monoclinic, penetration

twins or radiating aggregates
Hardness 4.5
Cleavage Distinct
Specific gravity 2.41-2.50
Colour Colourless, yellow, brown or pink
Lustre Vitreous
Refractive index 1.505-1.512
Streak White
Name From Greek words for join and cut, alluding to the shape of the twinned crystals

Found in cavities in basalts and related igneous rocks; fine crystals from Strontian, Argyll (Scotland). Also found near Ossining, New York (USA), Norway, Bodenmais, Bavaria and St Andreasberg (West Germany), and USSR.

Hauyne

$(NaCa)_{4-8}Al_6Si_6(O,S)_{24}(SO_4,Cl)_{1-2}$

Sodalite group

Aricca, Italy

Crystal system, form and habit Cubic forming dodecahedra or octahedra

Hardness 5.5-6
Cleavage Distinct
Specific gravity Near 2.4
Colour Bright blue
Lustre Vitreous to greasy
Refractive index Near 1.5
Streak Faint blue
Diaphaneity Transparent
Other features Some German material may fluoresce orange-red
Name From R J Hauy, French mineralogist

Hauyne is found in alkaline igneous rocks, notably from the Laacher See, Eifel (West Germany) where it occurs with leucite and nepheline. It is one of the constituents of lapis lazuli. Also from Somma, Vesuvius and Monte Albani (Italy).

Hedenbergite $CaFe^{2+}Si_2O_6$

Pyroxene group

Nordmark, Sweden

Crystal system, form and habit Monoclinic, short prismatic or massive
Hardness 6
Cleavage Perfect prismatic
Specific gravity 3.56
Colour Brownish to dark green
Lustre Vitreous to resinous or dull
Refractive index 1.716-1.751
Streak White or grey
Diaphaneity Transparent to translucent
Name From the Swedish chemist M A L Hedenberg

Found in limestone contact zones, iron-rich metamorphic rocks and in granites and other igneous rocks; translucent bright green manganous hedenbergite from New Broken Hill Consolidated mine, New South Wales (Australia). Forms a series with diopside.

Hematite αFe_2O_3

Hematite group

Gotthard, Switzerland

Crystal system, form and habit Trigonal; reniform masses, tabular crystals in rosettes
Hardness 5-6
Cleavage None; rhombohedral or basal parting
Specific gravity 5.26
Colour Steel-grey to iron black, red in thin section, often twinned
Lustre Metallic to dull
Refractive index 3.22-2.94
Streak Deep red
Diaphaneity Very thin plates transparent
Other features Sometimes shows iridescent tarnish
Name From Greek words meaning blood red, referring to its colour

Found in many places as the chief ore of iron and usually occurring in thick sedimentary beds though there are many other modes of formation. Fine reniform 'kidney ore' masses from Cumbria (England) and excellent crystals from Elba, Vesuvius and Etna, also Traversella, Piedmont (Italy). Also from the St Gotthard, and well-developed crystals from the Cavradischlucht, Tavetsch (Switzerland) Hair-like crystals from Emmelberg, Eifel (West Germany).

Hemimorphite

$Zn_4Si_2O_7(OH)_2.H_2O$

Iglesias, Sardinia

Crystal system, form and habit Orthorhombic, thin tabular or as fan-shaped aggregates,

hemimorphic
Hardness 4.5-5
Cleavage Perfect prismatic
Specific gravity 3.4-3.5
Colour White or pale blue'
Lustre Vitreous to silky
Refractive index 1.614-1.636
Streak Colourless
Diaphaneity Transparent to translucent
Other features Pale orange fluorescence LWUV, white SWUV
Name From the hemimorphic symmetry of the crystals

Found as a secondary mineral in the oxidized zone of ore deposits. Fine crystals from Mapimi, Durango (Mexico) and at Santa Eulalia, Chihuahua (Mexico); Stone mine , Leadville, Colorado (USA); Sunshine mine, Bingham, New Mexico (USA).

Herderite

$CaBe(PO_4)F$

Minas Gerais, Brazil

Crystal system, form and habit Monoclinic, stout prismatic, pseudo-orthorhombic; radial aggregates
Hardness 5-5.5
Cleavage Interrupted prismatic
Specific gravity 2.95-3.01
Colour Colourless to pale yellow or greenish-white
Lustre Vitreous
Refractive index 1.591-1.621

Diaphaneity Transparent to translucent
Other features Some specimens fluoresce deep blue LWUV

Name From S A W von Herder, a mining official from Saxony (East Germany)

Found in granite pegmatites, very rarely cut as a gemstone. Fine light yellow-brown crystals from Stoneham and other localities in Maine (USA). Very fine crystals from the Golconda mine, Governador Valadares (Mexico) and Virgem da Lapa (the variety hydroxyl-herderite). From Minas Gerais (Brazil) many crystals show fishtail twinning; also at Mursinsk (USSR).

Heulandite $(Na,Ca)_{2-3}Al_3(Al,Si)_2Si_{13}O_{36}.12H_2O$
Zeolite group

Berufjord, Iceland

tabular crystals, characteristically coffin-shaped
Hardness 3.5-4
Cleavage Perfect side pinacoidal
Specific gravity 2.2
Colour White, reddish or yellowish
Streak White
Diaphaneity Transparent to translucent
Name From the English mineral collector J H Heuland

Crystal system, form and habit Monoclinic, as elongated

Found with other zeolites in the trap rocks at Paterson, New Jersey (USA) and long ago from Berufjordhur (Iceland). Good red crystals from Gunnedah, and orange crystals from Gurawilla, New South Wales (Australia).

Hornblende
Amphibole group

$CaNa(Mg,Fe)_4(Al,Fe,Ti)_3Si_6O_{22}(O,OH)_2$

Ontario, Canada

Crystal system, form and habit Monoclinic short to long

prismatic
Hardness 5-6
Cleavage Prismatic
Specific gravity 3.0-3.4
Colour Green or bluish-green, yellow, brown to black
Lustre Vitreous
Diaphaneity Transparent to translucent
Name From German word meaning 'to deceive', alluding to the lack of valuable ores from the mineral

Found in igneous and metamorphic rocks. Large crystals from Franklin, New Jersey (USA) and from many European Alpine localities. Forms a rock known as amphibolite.

Howlite

$Ca_2B_5SiO_9(OH)_5$

California, USA

Crystal system, form and habit Monoclinic, nodular

masses
Hardness 3.5
Specific gravity 2.45-2.58
Colour White
Refractive index 1.583-1.605
Other features May fluoresce brownish-yellow SWUV, some Californian material glows deep orange LWUV
Name From H How who described a mineral with similar composition

Found in arid regions and borate deposits; frequently dyed blue to imitate turquoise. From Lang, Los Angeles County, California and from the Mohave Desert in the same state (USA).

Ilmenite

$Fe^{2+}TiO_3$

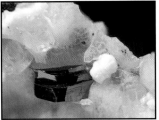

Mont St Hilaire, Quebec, Canada

Crystal system, form and habit Trigonal, equidimensional or tabular crystals; massive
Hardness 5-6
Specific gravity 4.1-4.8
Colour Black to brownish-black or deep red (variety pyrophanite)
Lustre Metallic
Streak Black to yellow or brownish-red
Name From the Ilmen Mountains (USSR)

Sharp crystals from pegmatite at Kragero (Norway). Flat plates from some occurrences in pegmatites in the USA at Litchfield, Massachusetts and also from Miask, Urals (USSR); Aschaffenburg (West Germany); from hydrothermal veins in the St Gotthard and Binnental (Switzerland); Bourg d'Oisans, Dauphiné (France).

Jadeite

$Na(Al,Fe^{3+})Si_2O_6$

Pyroxene group

Wyoming; California; Washington, USA
Crystal system, form and habit Monoclinic, as masses of

interlocking crystals and found as pebbles
Hardness 6.5-7
Specific gravity 3.33
Colour Emerald-green, green, yellow, lavender, grey
Refractive index Usually near 1.66
Other features Splintery fracture, very tough
Name From the Spanish piedra de ijada, referring to its power of healing kidney disorders

Jadeite is the brighter of the two minerals entitled to the name of jade (the other is nephrite). It is found in serpentine and is derived from olivine rocks but it is almost invariably recovered as pebbles or boulders in streams. The finest, emerald-green 'Imperial' jade, is translucent with no hint of white streakiness, and is found in veins with albite in a country rock of serpentine. The material described so far is from Upper Burma. Jadeite is also found in the Clear Creek area of San Benito County, California (USA) and there are deposits in Guatemala in the valley of the Rio Grande Motagua (USA).

Jamesonite

$Pb_4FeSb_6S_{14}$

Noche Buena, Zacatecas, Mexico

Crystal system, form and habit Monoclinic, fibrous or feathery masses
Hardness 2.5
Cleavage Across the elongation
Colour Dark grey
Lustre Metallic lustre
Name From Scottish mineralogist Robert Jameson

Found with lead ores at Pribram (Czechoslovakia); Trepca (Yugoslavia); Baia Sprei, Felsobanya (Romania); matted hair-like specimens from Cornwall (England); Idaho and Utah (USA). Fibres more brittle than those of boulangerite; also from Guangxi (China).

Kammererite

Chlorite group

Kop Daglari, Turkey

Hardness 2-2.5
Specific gravity 2.70
Colour Dark reddish-purple to lavender
Lustre Vitreous
Refractive index 1.588-1.594
Diaphaneity Translucent
Name From a Russian mining director A A Kammerer

Kammererite is a chromian variety of clinochlore and is found at the chromium mines at Kop Krom, Askale, Anatolia (Turkey); also as small crystals at Texas, Lancaster County, Pennsylvania (USA).

Kernite

$Na_2B_4O_6(OH)_2.3H_2O$

Boron, California, USA

Crystal system, form and habit Monoclinic, usually as masses with a fibrous structure

Hardness 2.5-3
Cleavage Perfect
Specific gravity 1.9
Colour Colourless altering to white
Lustre Dull to vitreous or pearly
Diaphaneity Transparent when fresh, altering to opaque
Other features Notably brittle and splintery
Name From Kern County California

Found in veins and as masses in playa deposits near Boron, Kern County, California (USA) and from the Tincalayu borax mine, Salta (Argentina).

Kornerupine

$Mg_3Al_6(Si,Al,B)_5O_{21}(OH)$

Greenland

Crystal system, form and habit Orthorhombic, columnar crystals

Hardness 6.5
Cleavage Perfect 2 directions
Specific gravity 3.28-3.34
Colour Dark brownish-green or bluish-green
Lustre Vitreous
Refractive index 1.665-1.682
Other features Bright apple-green vanadium kornerupine found in Kenya; some chatoyant material found in Sri Lanka
Name From A N Kornerup, Danish geologist

Kornerupine is usually found as water-worn pebbles in alluvial deposits though some pale blue transparent material has been found in the pegmatites of Madagascar. Sri Lanka and to some extent Burma provide most gem quality material.

Kyanite

Al_2SiO_5

Graves Mountain, Georgia, USA
Crystal system, form and habit Triclinic, flattened bladed crystals

Hardness 7.5 across length, 4.5 along length
Cleavage Perfect 1 pinacoidal
Specific gravity 3.68
Colour Blue to green
Lustre Vitreous to pearly
Refractive index 1.712-1.734
Diaphaneity Transparent to translucent
Other features Strongly pleochroic; may show Cr absorption spectrum
Name From a Greek word meaning blue

Trimorphous with sillimanite and andalusite, kyanite is a characteristic mineral of schists, gneisses and granite pegmatites. Fine crystals found at a number of places in the Alps including Pizzo Forno, Ticino (Switzerland) and from Pfitsch, Greiner and in the Stubai and Otztal Alps and the Hohe Tauern (Austria). Large clear crystals from Kenya. Reported from Sichuan, the Xinjiang Autonomous Region, and elsewhere in China. Transparent blue and green crystals from Minas Gerais (Brazil). Some material from Central Africa contains chromium and is an attractive blue-green.

Laumontite

$CaAl_2Si_4O_{12}.4H_2O$

Zeolite group

Bishop, California, USA
Crystal system, form and habit Monoclinic, usually square prisms with steep terminations,

often showing swallow-tail twins. Also fibrous, columnar and radiating
Hardness 3-4
Cleavage Perfect
Specific gravity 2.20-2.41
Colour White, grey, yellowish, pink or brownish
Lustre Vitreous to pearly
Streak Colourless
Name From the mineral's French discoverer F P N Gillet de Laumont

Found in cavities or veins in a variety of different rock types most commonly in basalts or pegmatites. Fine crystals from the Pine Creek tungsten mine, Bishop, California and from the trap rocks of New Jersey (USA). Also from Harzburg (West Germany); Plauenscher Grund, Saxony (East Germany); Zillertal, Tirol (Austria).

Lazulite $MgAl_2(PO_4)_2(OH)_2$

Lazulite group

Yukon, Canada

Crystal system, form and habit Monoclinic, forming solid masses but some wedge-shaped crystals
Hardness 5.5-6
Cleavage Poor
Specific gravity 3.1-3.4
Colour Bright to dark blue
Lustre Vitreous
Diaphaneity Transparent to translucent
Name From its colour

Lazulite is a high-temperature hydrothermal mineral found as good blue crystals in quartz veins at Zermatt (Switzerland) and in western Austria; some gem-quality fragments in pegmatite detritus from Minas Gerais (Brazil). Forms a series with scorzalite.

Lazurite Sodalite group
$(Na,Ca)_{7-8}(Al,Si)_{12}(O,S)_{24}[(SO_4),Cl_2,(OH)2(OH)_2]$

Afghanistan
Crystal system, form and habit Cubic, usually massive;

dodecahedral crystals, rare
Hardness 5-6
Cleavage Poor dodecahedral
Specific gravity 2.7-2.9
Colour Blue
Lustre Vitreous
Refractive index 1.5
Diaphaneity Translucent
Other features Some material, notably from Chile, shows patchy orange fluorescence from included calcite. Bad eggs smell if a drop of HCl placed on specimen.

Name From a Persian word for blue

Lazurite is a variety of hauyne with a high sulphur content. The ornamental material lapis lazuli is a rock composed of lazurite, hauyne, sodalite and nosean, all members of the sodalite group. Found as contact metamorphic minerals in limestones and granites. Finest material from the Sar-e-Sang mine, Jurm, Badakshan (Afghanistan). Also from San Bernardino, California (USA); western shore of Lake Baikal, Siberia (USSR); Coquimbo (Chile).

Leadhillite $Pb_4(SO_4)(CO_3)_2(OH)_2$

Grand Reef mine, Arizona, USA

Hardness 2.5
Cleavage Perfect, near micaceous
Specific gravity 6.3-6.4
Colour Pearly white, with tinges of yellow, blue or green.
Lustre Adamantine to pearly
Diaphaneity Translucent to transparent
Other features Slightly sectile. May fluoresce orange
Name From the locality, Leadhills, Lanarkshire (Scotland)

Crystal system, form and habit Monoclinic, usually platy crystals.

Found in the weathered zone of lead ore deposits. Attractive blue crystals from the Mammoth mine, Tiger, Arizona (USA); also from Leadhills, Lanarkshire (Scotland); from Grube Marie, Wilmsdorf, Siegerland (West Germany).

Legrandite

$Zn_2(AsO_4)(OH) \cdot H_2O$

Ojuela mine , Mapimi, Mexico
Crystal system, form and habit Monoclinic, long prismatic crystals sometimes aggregated in sprays or fans
Hardness 4.5
Cleavage Fair
Specific gravity 3.9
Colour Colourless to wax yellow
Lustre Vitreous
Refractive index 1.675-1.740
Diaphaneity Transparent to translucent
Name From M Legrand, Belgian mine manager

Found in cavities in limonite; with adamite at the Ojuela mine, Mapimi, Durango (Mexico).

Lepidolite

$K(Li,Al)_3(Si,Al)_4O_{10}(F,OH)_2$

Mica group

Little Three mine, California, USA
Crystal system, form and habit Monoclinic, usually as platy masses; tabular crystals fairly rare
Hardness 2.5-4
Cleavage Perfect basal, micaceous cleavage
Specific gravity 2.8-3.3
Colour Pearly. Lilac to purple
Diaphaneity Translucent to transparent
Name From a Greek word in allusion to its scaly nature

Found in granite pegmatites, lepidolite is sometimes used ornamentally. From Rozna, Moravia (Czechoslovakia); San Diego County, California (USA); Antsirabe (Madagascar); Elba (Italy). Well-formed crystals from Auburn, Maine (Canada). Large sheets from the Londonderry pegmatite (Australia).

Leucite

$KAlSi_2O_6$

Casserta, Italy
Crystal system, form and habit Tetragonal (pseudocubic) forming trapezohedral crystals

Hardness 5.5-6
Cleavage Poor dodecahedral
Specific gravity 2.47-2.5
Colour Colourless to yellowish
Lustre Vitreous or dull
Refractive index 1.5
Diaphaneity Translucent to transparent
Other features May show interference colours; some Italian material gives a bright orange fluorescence LWUV
Name From a Greek word for white

Leucite is found in K-rich basic lavas and is especially associated with the Alban Hills, Rome (Italy) where colourless crystals up to 0.5in/1cm are found. Some have been faceted. Also from the Laacher See, Eifel (West Germany); Magnet Cove, Arkansas (USA).

Libethenite

$Cu_2(PO_4)(OH)$

Phoenix mine, Cornwall, England
Crystal system, form and

habit Orthorhombic, forming equant to short prismatic crystals or as crusts
Hardness 4
Cleavage Two indistinct
Specific gravity 3.97
Colour Light to dark blackish-green or light to dark olive-green
Lustre Vitreous to greasy
Diaphaneity Transparent to translucent
Name From Libethen (Romania)

Found mainly as a secondary mineral in the oxidation zone of copper ore deposits. From the Inspiration and Castle Dome, Gila County, Arizona (USA); from the Phoenix mine, Linkinhorne, Cornwall (England); from Libethen, Neusohl (Romania).

Limonite

FeO(OH).nH$_2$O

Pennsylvania, USA

Crystal system, form and habit Amorphous
Specific gravity 2.7-4.3
Colour Black, brown, yellow
Lustre vitreous
Streak Yellow/brown
Name From the Greek word for meadows, alluding to limonite's occurrence in swampy terrain

Limonite is a general name given to hydrous iron oxides, mostly goethite or pepidocrocite. Found as an alteration product of iron-bearing minerals in all types of rocks and with a worldwide distribution.

Linarite

PbCu(SO$_4$)(OH)$_2$

Grand Reef mine, Arizona
Crystal system, form and habit Monoclinic, elongated or

tabular crystals
Hardness 2.5
Cleavage One perfect, one fair
Specific gravity 5.35
Colour Deep blue
Lustre Vitreous to sub-adamantine
Refractive index 1.80-1.85
Streak Pale blue
Diaphaneity Translucent to transparent
Name From Linares, a Spanish location

Found in the oxidized zone of copper and lead deposits. Fine crystals occur at Red Gill and Roughten Gill, Cumbria (England) and from Leadhills, Lanarkshire (Scotland). Fine specimens also from the Cerro Gordo mines, Inyo County, California (USA) in association with leadhillite and anglesite; long crystals up to 4in/10cm from the Mammoth mine, Tiger, Arizona (USA); also from the Sunshine mine, Bingham, New Mexico and from the Grand Reef mine, Graham County, Arizona (USA). Linarite is found with malachite at Grube Victoria, Littfeld, Siegerland and from Grube Friedrichsegen, Bad

Ems (West Germany). From Montevecchio (Sardinia), and Broken Hill, New South Wales (Australia).

Löllingite
$FeAs_2$
Löllingite group

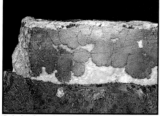

Cobalt, Ontario, Canada

Crystal system, form and habit Orthorhombic, usually massive, sometimes small prismatic crystals
Hardness 5-5.5
Cleavage Basal
Specific gravity 6.2-8.6
Colour Tin-white
Lustre Metallic lustre
Name From Lölling, Carinthia (Austria)

Found in high and medium-temperature veins and in pegmatites (the Fe-rich variety of the mineral). From Norway, Sweden and Finland; Franklin, New Jersey (USA), and from some New England pegmatites (USA).

Ludlamite
$(Fe^{2+},Mg,Mn)_3(PO_4)_2.4H_2O$

Santa Eulalia, Mexico
Crystal system, form and habit Monoclinic, thin to thick

wedge-shaped or as masses
Hardness 3.5
Cleavage Perfect
Specific gravity 3.2
Colour Bright to apple green or colourless
Lustre Vitreous
Refractive index 1.650-1.697
Diaphaneity Transparent to translucent
Name From the English mineralogist Henry Ludlam

Found in the oxidation zone of ore deposits and as an alteration of primary iron phosphates in granite pegmatites. Fine crystals from the Blackbird area, Lemhi County, Idaho (USA) and from Hagendorf, Bavaria (West Germany). From Santa Eulalia, Chihuahua (Mexico).

Magnesite

$MgCO_3$

Minas Gerais, Brazil

Crystal system, form and habit Trigonal; usually massive; some rhombs known

Hardness 3.5-4.5
Cleavage Perfect rhombohedral
Specific gravity 3.0-3.1
Colour Colourless to brown
Lustre Vitreous to dull
Refractive index 1.50-1.71
Diaphaneity Transparent to translucent
Other features Blue to green fluorescence, with some phosphorescence SWUV; effervesces in warm acids
Name From the composition

Magnesite occurs as an alteration product of Mg-rich rocks and in some sedimentary deposits and hydrothermal ore deposits. Fine rhombs are found at Brumado, Bahia (Brazil); also from India, Greece, USSR, Yugoslavia. Good crystals from Oberndorf, Styria (Austria).

Magnetite

$Fe^{2+}Fe^{3+}_2O_4$

Binntal, Switzerland

Crystal system, form and

habit Cubic, usually octahedra; commonly massive
Hardness 6
Cleavage None; octahedral parting
Specific gravity 5.2
Colour Black
Lustre Metallic
Streak Black
Other features Magnetic
Name From a district in Thessaly (Greece)

Magnetite is found in plutonic, pegmatitic and metamorphic rocks and in sands. It is an important ore of iron. From the Berliner Hutte, Zillertal (Austria); Elba (Italy); fine crystals from French Creek, Pennsylvania and from the zinc mines [franklinite] at Franklin, New Jersey (USA). Hematite pseudomorphs after magnetite commonly occur; Hubei [rhombdodecahedral] and Jiangsu [octahedral] crystals (China).

Malachite

$Cu_2(CO_3)(OH)_2$

Clifton, Arizona, USA

Crystal system, form and habit Monoclinic: rarely as single crystals; usually botryoidal masses; commonly twinned

Hardness 3.5-4
Cleavage Basal
Specific gravity 4.05
Colour Bright to dark green
Lustre Adamantine, silky or vitreous (crystals); dull (masses)
Refractive index 1.655-1.909
Streak Pale green
Diaphaneity Transparent to translucent
Other features Soluble in dilute acids
Name From a Greek word denoting its colour

Malachite is one of the ores of copper though not the most important one. It occurs in the upper oxidized zone of copper deposits. Fine material from the Demidoff mine, Nizhne-Tagilsk, Siberia (USSR) and fine pseudomorphs after cuprite are found at Chessy (France). Small groups of crystals are found in Cornwall (England) and fine large masses in the Bisbee area, Cochise County, Arizona (USA). It is also found in association with azurite to give azur-malachite; both this and malachite are frequently used ornamentally. Other important locations include Brixlegg and Mitterberg (Austria); West German locations include Rheinbreitbach, the Eifel region, Littfeld, Mechernich and Lichtenberg and the mineral has been found with cerussite at the Friedrich mine, Niederhövels, Siegerland. It has been found at Rudabanya (Hungary), the Tynagh mine (Irish Republic) and Laurium (Greece). Fine translucent micromount crystals from the Loudville lead mine, Massachusetts (USA). Good quality material from Bwana Mkubwa (Zambia) and Luishwishi, Katanga (Zaire).

Manganite

MnO(OH)

Ilfeld, Harz, West Germany

habit Monoclinic, well developed prisms with flat base
Hardness 4
Cleavage Perfect side, poor prismatic and basal
Specific gravity 4.2-4.4
Colour Steel grey to iron black
Lustre Submetallic
Streak Red-brown
Diaphaneity Translucent reddish-brown in thin splinters
Crystal system, form and
Name From its composition

Found in veins and with manganese ores, manganite is formed at higher temperatures than other manganese oxides. Fine crystals from Ilfeld, Harz (Germany) and from an iron mine at Negaunee, Michigan (USA); also from Guangxi (China).

Marcasite

FeS_2

Folkestone, England

Crystal system, form and
habit Orthorhombic, tabular or pyramidal crystals with curved faces
Hardness 6-6.5
Cleavage Poor prismatic
Specific gravity 4.85-4.88
Colour Pale brassy yellow with iridescence
Lustre Metallic lustre
Name From an Arabic or Moorish word

The marcasite of the jeweller is pyrite, the more stable form of iron disulphide. 'Cockscomb pyrite' is a name given to an aggregate of flattened twinned marcasite crystals. Marcasite forms at low temperatures, commonly in sedimentary environments and in low temperature veins. Worldwide occurrence; notably from Príbram (Czechoslovakia), Freiberg, Saxony (East Germany); Joplin, Missouri (USA). Dimorphous with pyrite. Note that specimens oxidize – a problem not yet overcome by curators. Sulphur is freed to form acids which attack surroundings.

Mendipite

$Pb_3Cl_2O_2$

Merehead quarry, Avon, England
Crystal system, form and habit Orthorhombic, forming columnar or fibrous masses, often radiating
Hardness 2.5
Cleavage Perfect
Specific gravity 7.24
Colour Colourless to grey with some yellow, blue or red, always pale
Lustre Adamantine to resinous on fractures, pearly on cleavages
Streak White
Name From the Mendip Hills (England)

Found with cerussite, pyromorphite, malachite, calcite and manganese oxides at Higher Pitts Farm and Churchill, Mendip Hills (England). Also from the Altai Mountains (USSR).

Microlite

$(Ca,Na)_2Ta_2O_6(O,OH,F)$

Alto Ligonha, Mozambique
Crystal system, form and habit Cubic, octahedral
Hardness 5-5.5
Cleavage None; octahedral parting
Specific gravity 4.2-6.4
Colour Yellow-brown to greenish-black
Lustre Resinous
Streak White, yellowish or brownish
Diaphaneity Translucent to transparent
Name From the Greek word for small, referring to the size of the crystals first discovered

Microlite forms a series with pyrochlore and is found in pegmatite dikes or in large calcite-rich intrusive masses. Fine crystals from pegmatites at Haddam Neck, Connecticut, Portland (USA); large yellow-brown or greenish-brown crystals from the Rutherford pegmatite, Amelia, Virginia (USA). Green crystals from Equador, Parelhas (Brazil).

Milarite

$K_2Ca_4Al_2Be_4Si_{24}O_{60}.H_2O$

Osumilite group

Jaguaracu, Minas Gerais, Brazil

habit Hexagonal prismatic
Hardness 5.5-6
Specific gravity 2.5
Colour Colourless, pale green or yellowish green
Lustre Vitreous
Diaphaneity Transparent to translucent
Name From Val Milar (Switzerland). But this was not the correct locality for the original specimens

Crystal system, form and

Fine crystals from the Valencia mine, Guanajuato (Mexico) and from various Alpine veins and pegmatites, including some from Brazil. Gem-quality crystals from Swakopmund (Namibia).

Millerite

NiS

Antwerp, New York, USA

Crystal system, form and habit Trigonal, hair-like crystals or crusts
Hardness 3-3.5
Cleavage 2 rhombohedral
Specific gravity 5.3-5.6
Colour Brass-yellow
Name From English mineralogist W H Miller

Characteristic capillary crystals from Keokuk, Iowa (USA) and also found with metallic sulphides in German veins; from Rio delle Marne, Parma (Italy).

Mimetite

$Pb_5(AsO_4)_3Cl$

Tsumeb, Namibia

Hardness 3.5-4
Cleavage Pyramidal
Specific gravity 7.24
Colour Bright orange to pale yellow
Lustre Vitreous
Diaphaneity Transparent to translucent
Other features Orange red fluorescence shown by some crystals from Tsumeb (Namibia)
Name From a Greek word meaning imitator, referring to the resemblance between mimetite and pyromorphite crystals

Crystal system, form and habit Monoclinic, pseudohexagonal, acicular or globular crystals though some well-formed prismatic crystals are known

Found as a secondary mineral in the oxidized zone of lead ore deposits. The name campylite is often given to orange-yellow rounded crystals from such British localities as Alston Moor and the Dry Gill mine, Carrock Fells, Cumbria. Pale brown prisms from Wheal Unity, Gwennap, Cornwall. Fine crystals in old collections often from Johanngeorgenstadt, Saxony (East Germany), and fine bright yellow crystals also from Grube Clara, Wolfach, Schwarzwald (West Germany). Very fine clear yellow to golden crystals also from Tsumeb (Namibia). White crystals from the Tynagh mine (Ireland). Fine orange crystals from the Kintore opencast, Broken Hill, New South Wales (Australia), and green crystals from the Elura mine, Cobar, New South Wales (Australia). 'Wheatsheaves' are found at the Rowley mine in the Painted Rock mountains of Arizona (USA). Good crystals from locations in Chihuahua (Mexico).

Molybdenite

MoS_2

Chelan, Washington, USA

Crystal system, form and

habit Hexagonal, thin to thick tabular or barrel-like prisms; usually as foliate masses or scales
Hardness 1-1.5
Cleavage Perfect micaceous basal
Specific gravity 4.62-5.06
Colour Lead grey
Lustre Metallic. Greasy feel
Streak Greenish
Other features Sectile
Name From its composition

Found widespread as the major ore of molybdenum. Occurs in high-temperature veins, contact metamorphic deposits, pegmatites and granites. Important deposit at the Climax mine, Lake County, Colorado (USA). Also from England; Knaben mine (Norway); Cinovec (Czechoslovakia); Bleiberg, Carinthia (Austria); Zhejiang and Liaoning (China); Radautal bei Bad Harzburg (Germany).

Monazite

$(Ce,La,Y,Th)(PO_4)$

Monazite group

New Mexico, USA

Crystal system, form and habit Monoclinic, small reddish-brown crystals, opaque and

flattened
Hardness 5-5.5
Cleavage One good, several poor
Specific gravity 4.9-5.3
Colour Brown
Lustre Adamantine to resinous
Streak Reddish to light yellowish-brown
Diaphaneity Transparent to translucent
Name From the Greek word for solitary, referring to the mineral's rarity

Crystals from pegmatites can be quite large (up to 4in/10cm across); these are typical of the deposit at Divino de Uba, Minas Gerais (Brazil). Similar crystals from Norwegian pegmatites especially from Gjerdingen. Alpine cavities contain clear golden crystals, particularly Tavetsch and Val Vigezzo (Switzerland); from Ossola, Novara (Italy).

Mottramite

$PbCu(VO_4)(OH)$

Tsumeb, Namibia

Crystal system, form and habit Orthorhombic, usually pyramidal or prismatic. Also found as aggregates or crystals, stalactites or coarse-fibred botryoidal masses

Hardness 3-3.5
Specific gravity 5.9
Colour Grass green to dark green
Lustre Vitreous to greasy
Streak Yellowish-orange to brownish-red
Diaphaneity Transparent to translucent
Name From Mottram St Andrew, Cheshire (England)

Found in the oxidation zone of ore deposits with other lead minerals. Found at Mottram St Andrew, Cheshire (England); at many places in Namibia, including Tsumeb; from the Mammoth mine, Tiger, Arizona (USA), and Crestmore, California (USA); also from Sardinia; Obir, Carinthia (Austria). Forms a series with descloizite.

Muscovite
Mica group

$KAl_2(Si_3Al)O_{10}(OH,F)_2$

Crystal Peak, Colorado, USA

Crystal system, form and habit Monoclinic, pseudohexagonal crystals, commonly lamellar masses or scaly

Hardness 2-2.5, varying with direction
Cleavage Perfect basal
Specific gravity 2.77-2.88
Colour Colourless, grey, brown, yellow, green, violet, rose or ruby red
Lustre Vitreous to pearly or silky
Streak colourless
Diaphaneity Translucent to transparent
Name From Muscovy glass, alluding to the Russian province of Muscovy

Found in a great number of different environments; very large crystals from some South Dakota pegmatites and from some Indian locations, especially the Inikurti mine, Nellore (India). Zoned green crystals near Salt Lake City, Utah (USA); from Xinjiang (China). Also from Alpine-type mineral veins in the St Gotthard (Switzerland) and Zillertal, Tirol (Austria). Large crystals also in pegmatites in Alice Springs (Australia); from northern Quebec and eastern Ontario (Canada).

Natrolite

$Na_2Ca_2Si_3O_{10}.2H_2O$

Zeolite group

Bergen Hill, New Jersey, USA

Crystal system, form and habit Orthorhombic, slender square needle-like crystals terminated by a 4-faced pyramid; massive fibrous
Hardness 5.5
Cleavage Perfect prismatic
Specific gravity 2.20-2.26
Colour Pearly; silky in fibrous varieties
Lustre White
Diaphaneity Transparent to translucent
Other features May show orange fluorescence LWUV
Name From its composition

Found in basaltic cavities and in other dark igneous rocks. Good material from Bound Brook, New Jersey (USA) can be faceted. From the Fassa Valley, South Tirol (Austria); Kimberley (South Africa); Teplice and Aussig (Czechoslovakia); Alpstein, Hesse (West Germany). From pegmatites at Mont St Hilaire, Quebec (Canada) and the Kola Peninsula (USSR); from Phillip Island, Victoria (Australia); Antronapiana, Ossola, Novara (Italy).

Nepheline

(Na,K)AlSiO$_4$

Vesuvius, Italy

Crystal system, form and habit Hexagonal, stumpy crystals; more commonly as grains in rock
Hardness 5.5-6

Cleavage Good prismatic
Specific gravity 2.55-2.66
Colour Colourless, greenish, blue, light to dark red
Lustre Vitreous to greasy
Refractive index 1.52-1.54
Diaphaneity Transparent to translucent
Other features Fluoresces medium light blue (German material) and dull orange (Ontario, Canada), both LWUV
Name From a Latin word for 'cloudy' in allusion to its cloudiness on immersion in acid

Nepheline is found in plutonic and volcanic rocks and in pegmatites associated with nepheline syenites. Specimens come from Julianehaab (Greenland), Langesundfjord (Norway); Monte Albani and Monte Somma, Vesuvius (Italy); Löbauerberg, Saxony (East Germany), and Katzenbuckel, Odenwald (West Germany); Larvin (Norway); Kola Peninsula (USSR). Large crystals from Bancroft, Ontario (Canada)

Nephrite
Amphibole group

Ca$_2$(Mg,Fe)$_5$(Si$_4$O$_{11}$)$_2$(OH)$_2$

New Zealand

Crystal system, form and habit Monoclinic, the fibrous variety of actinolite. Very tough from the felting together of

masses of fibrous crystals
Hardness 6-6-5
Specific gravity About 3
Colour Dark green, creamy-beige, yellow to brown
Refractive index Near 1.62
Other features Most archaic Chinese jade artefacts are nephrite which, with jadeite, is one of the minerals allowed the name jade.
Name From the Greek word for kidney with reference to the shape of the boulders

Found as boulders in streams; most nephrite of antiquity from the south and west of Sinkiang in eastern Turkestan and especially from the area of Khotan. From the Lake Baikal area of Siberia (USSR) and from Wyoming, California (USA), Alaska, and British Columbia (Canada); from New Zealand where it is highly prized by the Maori peoples and from Taiwan and New South Wales (Australia).

Neptunite

$KNa_2Li(Fe^{2+},Mn)_2Ti_2Si_8O_{24}$

San Benito County, California, USA

Crystal system, form and habit Monoclinic, prismatic with square cross-section

Hardness 5-6
Cleavage Perfect
Specific gravity 3.2
Colour Black with reddish-brown internal reflections
Lustre Vitreous
Streak Reddish-brown
Diaphaneity Nearly opaque
Name From Neptune, the Roman sea god, alluding to the mineral's occurrence with aegirine, itself named after the Scandinavian sea god

Found in San Benito County, California (USA); in pegmatites in Greenland and Ireland.

Norbergite

$Mg_3(SiO_4)(F,OH)_2$

Humite group

New Jersey, USA

Crystal system, form and habit Orthorhombic, highly

modified crystals or rounded grains
Hardness 6-6.5
Specific gravity 3.17
Colour Yellow to orange or brown
Lustre Vitreous to resinous
Diaphaneity Transparent to translucent
Other features May show yellow fluorescence
Name From Norberg (Sweden)

Found in contact zones in limestone or dolomite. From the Franklin area, Sussex County, New Jersey (USA); Ostanmosoa iron mine, Norberg (Sweden).

Northupite

$Na_3Mg(CO_3)_2Cl$

Uganda

Crystal system, form and habit Cubic, octahedra
Hardness 3.5-4
Specific gravity 2.38
Colour Colourless, yellowish or grey
Lustre Vitreous
Name From the American grocer C H Northup who first found the mineral

Found as good crystals at Searles Lake, San Bernardino County, California (USA).

Okenite

$Ca_5Si_9O_{23}.9H_2O$

Poona, India

Crystal system, form and habit Triclinic, usually as fibrous masses resembling puffballs
Hardness 4.5-5
Cleavage Perfect
Specific gravity 2.33
Colour White sometimes tinged with yellow
Lustre Vitreous to pearly
Name From German naturalist L Oken

Found in amygdules in basalts. From Iceland, the Faroe Islands, Chile, Disco Island (Greenland). Fine specimens from the Syhadree Mountains, Bombay (India).

Olivenite

$Cu_2AsO_4(OH)$

Wheal Unity, Gwennap, Cornwall, England

Crystal system, form and

habit Orthorhombic, forming small prismatic crystals or long slender prisms; or silky crusts of fibres.
Hardness 3
Cleavage 2, indistinct
Specific gravity 3.9-4.4
Colour Pistachio green to greenish-black
Lustre Adamantine to silky
Diaphaneity Translucent to opaque
Name From its colour

Found in the upper zone of copper deposits, associated with malachite, azurite, cerussite and cuprite. Crusts of needles found on some mine dumps in Cornwall (England) where the mines Wheal Unity, Wheal Jewel and Wheal Muttrell, Gwennap, were producers when working. Much of the Cornish material is colour-zoned. Found in West Germany at Reichenbach, Odenwald and Grube Clara, Schwarzwald. Found in old Arizona copper mines, particularly the New Cornelia mine, Ajo. Green translucent and bright-coloured zincian olivenite from the Kintore opencut, Broken Hill, New South Wales (Australia). Forms a series with adamite.

Olivine

$Mg_2SiO_4-Fe_2SiO_4$

Olivine group

St Johns Island, Egypt

Crystal system, form and habit Orthorhombic; usually found as water-worn pebbles; rare crystals show striated faces
Hardness 6.5-7

Cleavage Two directions
Specific gravity 3.22-4.29 for whole range; gem peridot 3.34
Colour Forsterite pale green to yellow; fayalite green to brown; gem peridot is olive green
Lustre Vitreous, slightly oily
Refractive index Group as a whole has 1.635-1.879; gem peridot 1.65-1.69
Diaphaneity Transparent to translucent
Other features Coloured by ferrous iron
Name From its colour

The olivine group consists of orthorhombic silicates, forsterite (Mg silicate) and fayalite (Fe silicate) forming end-members of an isomorphous series in which the gem variety peridot can be found. The olivines are found most commonly in basic igneous rocks and some basalts are mined for peridot. Gem peridot can be recognized when cut by its strong birefringence and from the presence of a distinctive absorption spectrum with bands at 490, 470 and 450nm. Burma, the Island of St John, and Arizona (USA) provide much of the finest gem peridot though some Hawaiian material is a bright green from chromium. Forsterite occurs in altered magnesian limestones but fayalite is found mostly contained within the natural glass obsidian. Crystals also from Forstberg and Mosenberg, Eifel (West Germany); Kraubath, Styria (Austria).

Opal

$SiO_2.nH_2O$

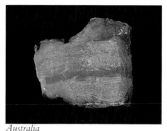

Australia

Crystal system, form and habit Amorphous, the play of spectrum colour being a diffraction effect from the three-dimensional array formed by the stacking of silica spheroids

Hardness 5.5-6.5

Specific gravity 2.1

Colour White and black opal describe the background seen behind the play of colour; water opal is nearly transparent; fire opal orange to red with or without a play of colour

Refractive index Near 1.45

Other features Some opals are green from nickel and do not show a play of colour. Others give a greenish fluorescence, probably from uranium

Name From the Sanskrit upala

Found in veins in sandstone in several places in Australia; Mexico (fire and water opals) from siliceous volcanic lavas and in rhyolites. From Honduras, Guatemala and Brazil (where it is found in a quartzitic sandstone); fine examples of opal pseudomorphs after wood from Humboldt County, Nevada (USA); from Czechoslovakia.

Orpiment

As_2S_3

Allchar, Macedonia, Greece

Crystal system, form and habit Monoclinic, prismatic crystals or compact masses with yellow flakes
Hardness 1.5-2.0
Cleavage Perfect micaceous
Specific gravity 3.4-3.5
Colour Orange, yellow to brown
Lustre Resinous and pearly
Diaphaneity Translucent to transparent
Other features Sectile and flexible but inelastic
Name From the Latin auripigmentum, alluding to its colour and early use

From Luceram (France) and Romania; Valilo (Iran) where it forms resinous brown crusts. Large crystals from Mercur, Utah (USA); rich masses from Getchell gold mine dumps, Nevada (USA); Jozankei, Hokkaido (Japan); Tajowa (Hungary); Raca Luchumi, South Caucasus (USSR).

Pargasite

$NaCa_2(Mg,Fe^{2+})_4Al(Si_6Al_2)O_{22}(OH)_2$

Amphibole group

California, USA

Crystal system, form and habit Monoclinic, short to long prismatic or massive, commonly twinned
Hardness 5-6
Cleavage Perfect
Specific gravity 3.07-3.18
Colour Light brown, green, grey to black
Lustre Vitreous
Name From Pargas (Finland)

Found in igneous and metamorphic rocks. From Pargas (Finland), and the Twin Lakes area of Fresno County, California (USA).

Pectolite

$NaCa_2Si_3O_8OH$

Bergen Hill, New Jersey, USA

Crystal system, form and habit Triclinic, mamillary masses

or needle-like crystals
Hardness 4.5-5
Cleavage Perfect but crumbles into fibres
Specific gravity 2.74-2.88
Colour Colourless to pale blue
Lustre Vitreous or silky
Diaphaneity Translucent
Other features Fluoresces orange LWUV
Name From a Greek word for compact, referring to its structure

Found in cavities in basaltic rock often with zeolites. A pale to medium blue translucent variety is used ornamentally under the name Larimar; it occurs in the Dominican Republic. Speci-Specimens from the New Jersey traprocks (USA). Avoid handling – crystals may penetrate the skin.

Periclase

MgO

Periclase group

Stassfurt, East Germany

Crystal system, form and habit Cubic, octahedral

Hardness 5.5
Cleavage One perfect
Specific gravity 3.56
Colour Colourless, grey, yellow, green
Lustre Vitreous
Refractive index 1.736
Streak White
Other features Pale yellow fluorescence LWUV for material from Terlingua (Texas)
Name From a Greek word in allusion to the cleavage

Periclase is found in marbles which have been contact metamorphosed-glassy grains can be found in the lava rocks of Vesuvius (Italy) and crystals are also found at Terlingua (Texas).

Perovskite

CaTiO$_3$

Perovskite group

Crystal system, form and habit Orthorhombic, pseudocubic crystals often twinned
Hardness 5.5
Cleavage Imperfect
Specific gravity 4.01
Colour Black, amber to yellow
Lustre Adamantine to metallic
Streak Colourless to pale grey
Name From the Russian mineralogist Count L A von Perovski

Oka District, Quebec, Canada

Found as an accessory mineral in ultrabasic and basic alkaline rocks, in schists or in contact metamorphosed limestones. Fine crystals from the benitoite mine, San Benito County, California (USA); fine crystals also from Magnet Cove, Arkansas (USA) and from the Zermatt area of Switzerland, also from the Zlatoust area, Ural Mountains (USSR); also from Lazio (Italy).

Petalite

LiAlSi$_4$O$_{10}$

Crystal system, form and habit Monoclinic, usually found as masses but some prismatic crystals are facetable
Hardness 6-7
Cleavage Perfect
Specific gravity 2.3-2.5
Colour Colourless to pale yellow
Refractive index 1.503-1.523
Diaphaneity Transparent
Name From the Greek word for leaf, in allusion to its cleavage

Elba, Italy

Found in granite pegmatites, most commonly from Brazil (most transparent specimens); also from Zimbabwe.

Pharmacosiderite $KFe^{3+}_4(AsO_4)_3(OH)_4.6\text{-}7H$

Cornwall, England

Crystal system, form and habit Cubic, 1 cube usual
Hardness 2.5
Cleavage Imperfect to good
Specific gravity 2.79
Colour Olive to emerald-green, amber to dark brown
Lustre Adamantine to greasy
Name From the Greek words for poison and for iron

Found as an oxidation product of arsenic-rich minerals, sometimes in hydrothermal deposits or pegmatites. Many locations in Cornwall (England); in pegmatites from the White Elephant mine, Custer County, South Dakota and from the Myler mine, Majuba Hill, Pershing County, Nevada (USA). From Reichenbach, Odenwald (West Germany); Cetine, Siena (Italy).

Phenakite Be_2SiO_4

Minas Gerais, Brazil
Crystal system, form and habit Trigonal, rhombohedral

crystals, often twinned
Hardness 7.5-8
Cleavage Poor prismatic
Specific gravity 2.93-3
Colour Colourless to wine, yellow, pinkish
Lustre Vitreous
Refractive index 1.65-1.67
Diaphaneity Transparent to translucent
Name From the Greek word for deceiver, alluding to the mineral's being mistaken for quartz

Found in granite pegmatites, hydrothermal veins and in Alpine-type deposits. From a number of locations in the state of Minas Gerais (Brazil), notably San Miguel di Piracicaba; from locations on the Takowaya river, Ural Mountains (USSR) and from Alpine deposits in Switzerland and Austria; fine bluish crystals from Lago Bianco, Ticino (Switzerland) and from Böckstein (Austria); Drammen (Norway). Good specimens from Mt Antero, Colorado (USA).

Phillipsite

$(K,Na,Ca)_{1-2}(Si,Al)_8O_{16}.6H_2O$

Zeolite group

Connecticut, USA

Crystal system, form and habit Monoclinic, forms inter-penetrant twins
Hardness 4-4.5
Cleavage Distinct
Specific gravity 2.2
Colour Colourless sometimes with reddish tinge
Lustre Vitreous
Name From British mineralogist William Phillips

Found like many zeolites in cavities in basalt and related rocks or from saline lake deposits or hot springs deposits. From saline lakes in California (USA); fine crystals from Capo di Bove (Italy); Stempel, Marburg and Sasbach am Kaiserstuhl (West Germany); several locations in Bohemia (Czechoslovakia).

Phlogopite

$KMg_3Si_3AlO_{10}(F,OH)_2$

Mica group

Burgess, Ontario, Canada

Crystal system, form and habit Monoclinic platy or scaly; crystals tapered prismatic
Hardness 2-2.5
Cleavage Perfect basal

Specific gravity 2.76-2.90
Colour Yellowish-brown to brownish-red
Lustre Pearly or submetallic on cleavage surfaces
Streak Colourless, may be tribo-luminescent
Diaphaneity Translucent
Other features May show 6 or 12 rayed star round distant light source when viewed through thin sheet
Name From the Greek word for fire-like, alluding to a reddish tinge shown on some specimens

Usually found in metamorphosed limestones and ultrabasic rocks. Large pseudohexagonal crystals from locations in Quebec (Canada). Also from Sweden; Sydenham, Ontario (Canada); Pargas (Finland); Fassa Valley, Tirol (Austria);

Madagascar; Sri Lanka. Good crystals from Franklin, New Jersey (USA); from Xinjiang (China). Forms a series with biotite.

Phosgenite

$Pb_2(CO_3)Cl_2$

Wallclose mine, Derbyshire, England

Crystal system, form and habit Tetragonal, prismatic; long and slender or short and square when large
Hardness 2-3 directional
Cleavage Good prismatic, poor basal
Specific gravity 6.1
Colour Yellowish to brown or colourless
Lustre Adamantine
Refractive index 2.11-2.14
Diaphaneity Transparent to translucent
Other features Weak yellowish fluorescence LWUV: soluble in and effervesces with dilute HNO_3
Name From phosgen, a name given to carbonyl chloride as phosgenite contains carbon, oxygen and chlorine

Phosgenite is formed when galena and other lead minerals are altered under surface conditions. Usually found with cerussite and anglesite. Fine crystals from Monteponi (Sardinia) and also found at Laurium (Greece) where sea water acting upon ancient lead slags caused it to form with laurionite. Occurs as large crystals with matlockite at Matlock, Derbyshire (England). Several Arizona (USA) locations contain phosgenite partly altered to cerussite.

Phosphophyllite

$Zn_2(Fe^{2+}Mn)(PO_4)_2.4H_2O$

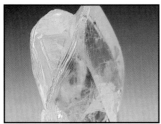

Potosi, Bolivia

Crystal system, form and habit Monoclinic, well developed crystals often with fishtail-shaped twins
Hardness 3.5
Cleavage Perfect frontal
Specific gravity 3.1
Colour Light blue green
Lustre Pearly white
Other features Soluble in acids
Name From its composition and its perfect cleavage

Fine gem-quality crystals from the tin mines at Potosi (Bolivia).
Also from Hagendorf, Bavaria (West Germany) where it is
found in pockets in greisen-like mica masses – or was until
recently. From the Palermo mine, North Groton, New
Hampshire (USA).

Platinum Pt

Ural Mountains, USSR

**Crystal system, form and
habit** Cubic, octahedra and
cubes or grains
Hardness 4-4.5
Specific gravity 14-19
Colour Light greyish-white
Lustre Metallic
Other features Malleable and
ductile. Sometimes magnetic
Name From the Spanish word
for silver

Found in placer deposits, often with gold. Primary occurrence
in basic igneous rocks. From Rustenburg, Bushveld (South
Africa); Sudbury (Canada) where it is found mostly as sper-
rylite. Finest crystals from placer deposits at Nizhne-Tagilsk,
Ural Mountains (USSR); also Choco (Colombia).

Pollucite $(Cs,Na)_2Al_2Si_4O_{12}.H_2O$

Namibia

**Crystal system, form and
habit** Cubic, cubes; usually fine-
grained masses
Hardness 6.5-7
Specific gravity 2.93
Colour Colourless, grey, occa-
sionally with pale tints of colour
Lustre Vitreous
Refractive index 1.52
Name From Pollux in Greek
mythology

Found in granite pegmatites. Forms a series with analcime.

Polybasite

$(Ag,Cu)_{16}Sb_2S_{11}$

Las Chiapas mine, Arizpe, Mexico

Crystal system, form and habit Monoclinic, forming flat pseudohexagonal plates
Hardness 2-3
Cleavage Perfect basal
Specific gravity 6.0-6.2
Colour Iron black, deep red and translucent in thin splinters
Lustre Metallic
Other features Fuses easily
Name From Greek words for many and base, alluding to the many metallic bases in its composition

Found with other silver antimony sulphides in low temperature silver veins. From Mexico and the German silver mines, particularly the Himmelsfurst mine, Freiberg (East Germany). Also from Grube Clara, Schwarzwald (West Germany). An ore of silver.

Polyhalite

$K_2Ca_2Mg(SO_4)_4.2H_2O$

Austria

Crystal system, form and

Crystal system, form and habit Triclinic, massive
Hardness 3.5
Cleavage One direction
Specific gravity 2.8 but water-solubility affects values
Colour Colourless, pale to brick-red
Lustre Resinous
Other features Bitter taste
Name From Greek words for many and salt, alluding to the several salts in its composition

Found in commercial salt deposits. Carlsbad (New Mexico); Hallstatt (Austria); Stassfurt (East Germany); Galicia (Poland).

Powellite

$CaMoO_4$

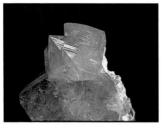

Marahastra, India

Crystal system, form and habit Tetragonal, forming thin yellowish films and plates with altered molybdenite
Hardness 3.5-4
Cleavage Bipyramidal
Specific gravity 4.2
Colour Yellowish
Diaphaneity Transparent to translucent
Other features Yellow fluorescence
Name From the American geologist J W Powell

Forms a series with scheelite and usually occurs from the alteration of molybdenite. May also be found in quartz veins or with zeolites. Finest crystals found long ago at Isle Royale, Michigan (USA). Also from Scotland and India, particularly from the Nasik district on the eastern flank of Pandulena Hill.

Prehnite

$Ca_2Al_2Si_3O_{10}(OH)_2$

Paterson, New Jersey, USA

Crystal system, form and habit Orthorhombic, crystals tabular but usually found as compact botryoidal masses
Hardness 6-6.5
Cleavage Distinct basal
Specific gravity 2.90-2.95
Colour Pale to dark green, yellow, grey to colourless
Lustre Vitreous to pearly
Streak Colourless
Diaphaneity Translucent to near-transparent
Name From the Dutch soldier Hendrik von Prehn who first collected the mineral

Found as a second stage mineral in cavities in basic igneous rocks, also in gneiss, granite and metamorphosed limestones. Fine crystals are found in European Alpine locations; from the traprocks of New Jersey (USA), particularly at Paterson and Bergen Hill, and from Crestmore, California (USA); Fassa Valley and Seiser Alm, Tirol (Austria); Haslach, Schwarzwald

(West Germany); Bourg d'Oisans, Dauphiné (France); Monte-catini (Italy); Jeffrey mine, Asbestos, Quebec (Canada).

Proustite

Ag_3AsS_3

Freiberg, Saxony, East Germany

Crystal system, form and habit Trigonal, prismatic or rhombohedral crystals, some-times scalenohedra; usually massive; twinning common
Hardness 2-2.5
Cleavage Distinct rhombohedral
Specific gravity 5.55-5.64
Colour Scarlet to vermilion
Lustre Adamantine to metallic
Streak Bright red
Diaphaneity Translucent to transparent
Other features Acquires tarnish on long exposure to light
Name From French chemist J L Proust

Proustite is found in low-temperature hydrothermal vein deposits. Fine bright red crystals come from the Dolores mine, Chanarcillo (Chile) and crystals of a darker red from Freiberg, Saxony (East Germany). Also from Ste Marie-aux-Mines (France), Wittichen, Schwarzwald and St Andreasberg, Harz (West Germany); Jachymov (Czechoslovakia); Cobalt, Ontario (Canada); and from several places in Mexico.

Pyrargyrite

Ag_3SbS_3

Ouray, Colorado, USA

Crystal system, form and habit Trigonal, prismatic, scalenohedral; usually massive
Hardness 2.5
Cleavage Distinct rhombohedral
Specific gravity 5.85
Colour Deep red
Lustre Adamantine to submetal-lic
Streak Dark red
Name From the Greek words for fire and silver alluding to its colour and composition

Found in low-temperature hydrothermal vein deposits with other sulphosalts and silver. Very fine crystals from localities in the Harz Mountains and from Teufelsgrund, Munstertal (West Germany). Also from Príbram (Czechoslovakia), Hiendelaencina (Spain); Ste Marie-aux-Mines, Alsace and Chalanches, Isère (France) and Montevecchio (Sardinia). From the Valenciana mine, Guanajuato (Mexico) and Chanarcillo (Chile).

Pyrite
FeS$_2$

Pyrite group

Crystal system, form and habit Cubic, forming cubes and pyritohedra; faces striated
Hardness 6-6.5
Specific gravity 5.0-5.3
Colour Brassy yellow
Streak Greenish-black
Name From the Greek word for fire, as it sparks when struck with steel

French Creek, Pennsylvania, USA

Found worldwide in a variety of environments. Pyrite is the 'marcasite' of the jeweller. Very fine crystals from Elba, Brosso and Traversella, Piedmont (Italy). Dimorphous with marcasite in several places. From the Tirolean Alps of Austria and from the Virtuous Lady mine, Buckland Monachorum, Devon (England). Fine crystals from Quiruvilca (Peru).

Pyrolusite
MnO$_2$

Crystal system, form and habit Tetragonal, long to short prismatic, commonly massive
Hardness 6-6.5
Specific gravity 5.06
Colour Black or dark grey
Lustre Metallic to dull
Diaphaneity Opaque

Utah, USA

Pyrolusite occurs as a secondary mineral from the alteration of manganite or other Mn-bearing minerals. It has a large distribution worldwide.

Pyromorphite

Pb₅(PO₄)₃Cl

$Pb_5(PO_4)_3Cl$

Apatite group

Wheatley mine, Pennsylvania, USA

Crystal system, form and habit Hexagonal, forming short

hexagonal prisms
Hardness 3.5-4
Cleavage Prismatic
Specific gravity 6.5-7.1
Colour Dark to yellow-green
Lustre Resinous lustre
Diaphaneity Translucent
Name From Greek words for fire and form, alluding to the crystalline state the mineral takes on cooling from fusion

Crystals which are often cavernous are found as secondary minerals in oxidized lead deposits. From the Bwlch-Glas mine (Wales), and from Wheal Alfred, Phillack, Cornwall and Roughten Gill, Cumbria (England); from Leadhills, Lanarkshire (Scotland). Fine crystals from Beresovsk (USSR); Mies (Yugoslavia); Príbram (Czechoslovakia); Clausthal, Bad Ems, Hofgrund and on azurite from Grube Phillipseck, Munster, Taunus, Hesse (West Germany). From Fieberbrunn, Tirol (Austria); Les Farges, Ussel (France) and Pfahl, Bavaria (West Germany). Fine bright yellow crystals from the Block 14 lease, Broken Hill, New South Wales (Australia); also from the Black Star opencast, Mount Isa mine, Queensland. Fine crystals from the Coeur d'Alene district, Idaho (USA).

Pyrope

Mg₃Al₂(SiO₄)₃

$Mg_3Al_2(SiO_4)_3$

Garnet group

Norway

Crystal system, form and

habit Cubic, forming rhombic dodecahedra, icositetrahedra or combinations; sometimes as formless lumps
Hardness 7-7.5
Specific gravity 3.5-3.8
Colour Pink to purplish-red, sometimes similar to ruby red
Lustre Vitreous
Refractive index 1.714
Name From Greek word for fiery from its colour

Pyrope forms an isomorphous series with almandine and is found in peridotites and serpentinites, particularly the diamond-bearing peridotites of southern Africa. Small bright stones with a small chromium content are known as Bohemian garnet from their original location in Eastern Europe. Most specimens used as gemstones come from India or the countries of East Africa; a lilac variety (rhodolite) from Cowee Creek, North Carolina (USA). Forms a series with almandine.

Pyrophyllite $Al_2Si_4O_{10}(OH)_2$

Graves Mountain, Georgia, USA

foliated masses
Hardness 1-2
Cleavage Perfect micaceous
Specific gravity 2.65-2.90
Diaphaneity Translucent to opaque
Other features The variety agalmatolite may show weak cream to white fluorescence LWUV (this material from China). Soapy feel
Name From Greek words for fire and leaf, referring to its exfoliation when heated

Crystal system, form and habit Monoclinic and triclinic forming tabular crystals or

Found in schists or in hydrothermal veins with quartz. The so-called South African wonderstone is dark grey; carvings have been made from North Carolina material. Coarse crystalline masses on quartz crystals found at Lincoln County, Georgia (USA).

Pyroxmangite $MnSiO_3$

Honshu, Japan

Crystal system, form and habit Triclinic; tabular crystals or masses; often twinned
Hardness 5.5-6
Cleavage Perfect 2 directions
Specific gravity 3.61-3.80
Colour Reddish-brown to pink
Lustre Vitreous to pearly
Refractive index 1.72-1.76
Diaphaneity Translucent to transparent

Name From its composition   pyroxene
Once thought to be Mn-bearing

Found in manganese-rich metamorphic rocks. Reddish-brown material from Kern County, California (USA), Scotland and Sweden. Some reddish material from Honshu (Japan) has been faceted, as has material from Broken Hill, New South Wales (Australia) where it occurs with rhodonite.

Pyrrhotite

$Fe_{1-x}S$

Santa Eulalia, Mexico

Crystal system, form and habit Monoclinic and hexagonal, tabular to platy steep or flat pyramidal
Hardness 3.5-4.5
Cleavage None; basal parting
Specific gravity 4.69
Colour Bronze-yellow to brown
Lustre Metallic
Streak Dark greyish black
Other features Metallic: magnetic of varying intensity; iridescence on tarnish
Name From a Greek word meaning reddish

Pyrrhotite is found mainly in basic igneous rocks with other sulphides. Fine large crystals from Kisbanya, Transylvania (Romania) and from Val Passiria, Trentino (Italy). Very large crystals from the Morro Velho gold mine, Minas Gerais (Brazil). Occurs at a number of mines in the western United States; Kongsberg (Norway); Siegerland and Andreasberg (West Germany); large well-formed crystals from the San Antonio mine, Aquiles Serdan, Chihuahua (Mexico); Trepca (Yugoslavia); from Hunan (China).

Quartz

SiO$_2$

Guerrero, Mexico

**Crystal system, form and
habit** Trigonal, forming prisms
capped with rhombohedra, often
twinned; left- and right-handed
individuals recognizable.
Chalcedony is the massive form
and is fibrous in parallel bands.
Chert, flint and jasper are also
massive and crypto-crystalline
but do not show the distinct
banding of chalcedony
Hardness 7
Cleavage Not very perceptible
Specific gravity 2.651
Colour Colours include rose
quartz, amethyst (purple to
violet) citrine (yellow to golden)
smoky. Aventurine quartz is
green from included fuchsite.
Chalcedonies have a wide variety
of patterns and names; agates are
banded as is onyx. Jasper is
usually dark reddish-brown,
yellow or dark green
Lustre Vitreous
Refractive index 1.544-1.553
Name From a Saxon word
meaning cross-vein ore

Found in very many types of environment and from almost
every country. Fine amethyst from Brazil, USSR, Uruguay and
Mexico, among other places; Brazil and Madagascar provide
fine rose quartz crystals; some of these show 6-rayed stars. Citrine from Brazil or from heating amethyst. Fine commercial
chalcedony mostly from Brazil or Idar-Oberstein (Germany).
Amethyst also from Cornwall (England) for example from
Lower Bostrace pit, St Just; also from the Löffelhorn (Switzerland); Osilo (Sardinia).

Raspite

PbWO$_4$

Broken Hill, Australia

**Crystal system, form and
habit** Monoclinic, usually tabular
Hardness 2.5-3
Cleavage One perfect
Specific gravity 8.46
Colour Yellowish-brown
Lustre Adamantine
Refractive index 2.27-2.30
Streak Colourless
Other features Decomposed by
HCl
Name From the discoverer Rasp

Dimorphous with stolzite, raspite is found as small crystals in the gold placers of Sumidouro, Minas Gerais (Brazil) and in tin veins on the Cerro Estano, Guanajuato (Mexico).

Realgar

AsS

Washington, USA

Crystal system, form and habit Monoclinic, short prismatic often twinned

Hardness 1.5-2
Cleavage Perfect side, fair basal
Specific gravity 3.56
Colour Red to orange-yellow
Lustre Resinous to greasy
Refractive index 2.53-2.70
Streak Orange to red
Diaphaneity Translucent to transparent
Other features Decomposed by HNO_3 and by long exposure to light; sectile
Name From an Arabic phrase meaning powder of the mine

Realgar is found in low-temperature hydrothermal veins associated with lead and silver ores. Fine facetable crystals from the Reward mine, King County, Washington and at the Getchell mine, Nevada (USA); from Felsobanya, Nagyag and Cavnic (Romania); Binntal, Valais (Switzerland); Tajowa (Czechoslovakia); Vesuvius, Solfatara, Cetine, Siena (Italy) and Matra (Corsica). Fine crystals from Rollenberg bei Bruchsal, Baden-Wurttemberg (West Germany) and very fine crystals from Hunan (China). From Emet (Turkey) and Sarajevo (Yugoslavia).

Rhodochrosite

MnCO$_3$

Calcite group

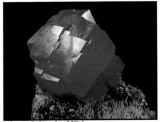

Alma, Colorado, USA

Crystal system, form and habit Trigonal; usually massive but fine scalenohedra also found

Hardness 3.5-4
Cleavage Perfect rhombohedral
Specific gravity 3.7
Colour Orange-pink or rose
Lustre Vitreous inclining to pearly
Refractive index 1.816-1.597
Streak White
Diaphaneity Transparent to translucent
Other features Soluble with effervescence in warm acids
Name From two Greek words describing its colour

Fine dark orange-pink crystals from the Kalahari manganese mines (South Africa); Cavnic (Romania); from Freiberg, Saxony (East Germany) and from the Wolf mine , Herdorf, Siegerland and from Rheinbreitbach (West Germany); Les Cabesses, Pyrenees (France); Madem Laccos (Greece) and the province of Huelva (Spain). From the Huallapon mine, Pasto Bueno (Peru); from Leadville and from the Home Sweet Home mine, Alma, Colorado (USA). From Trepca (Yugoslavia) and the Oppu mine (Japan). Forms a series with calcite and with siderite.

Rhodonite

(Mn,Fe,Mg)SiO$_3$

Broken Hill, New South Wales, Australia

Crystal system, form and habit Triclinic; tabular or massive

Hardness 5.5-6.5
Cleavage Perfect prismatic
Specific gravity 3.67 (crystals)
Colour Rose-red to pink
Lustre Vitreous
Refractive index 1.72-1.73
Diaphaneity Transparent to translucent
Other features Dull deep red fluorescence LWUV (Langban material); Mn absorption spectrum
Name From a Greek word for rose

Rhodonite is often used ornamentally and is found as masses with black veining of manganese oxides. It occurs in manganese-bearing ore bodies. Rhodonite is found in calcite at Franklin, New Jersey and in iron ore beds at Langban (Sweden) and also as fine small crystals at the Pajsberg iron mines near Filipstad (Sweden). Massive rhodonite is found in the Urals (USSR). From Broken Hill, New South Wales (Australia), where it is found with galena.

Rosasite

$(Cu,Zn)_2(CO_3)(OH)_2$

Rosasite group

Silver Bill mine, Arizona, USA

Crystal system, form and habit Monoclinic, botryoidal or mamillary crusts
Hardness 4.5
Cleavage 2 directions at right angles
Specific gravity 4.1
Colour Bluish-green
Diaphaneity Translucent
Name From the Rosas mine, Sulcis, Sardinia

Found as a secondary mineral in the oxidation zone of zinc-copper-lead deposits. From Mapimi, Durango (Mexico) as fine crystals and from the Silver Bill mine, Arizona and, with smithsonite, from Cerro Gordo, Inyo County, California (USA).

Roselite

$Ca_2(Co,Mg)(AsO_4)_2.2H_2O$

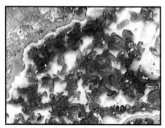

Schneeberg, Saxony, East Germany

Crystal system, form and habit Monoclinic, small poorly-formed crystals or crusts
Hardness 3.5
Cleavage Side pinacoidal
Specific gravity 3.5-3.7
Colour Deep rose pink
Lustre Vitreous
Streak Pink
Diaphaneity Transparent to translucent
Name From German mineralogist Gustav Rose

Found in the oxidized zone of cobalt-arsenide-rich ore veins. First finds from Schneeberg, Saxony (East Germany) – always twinned crystals from this location; also from Bou Azzer (Morocco) where it is found with erythrite.

Rutile

TiO$_2$

Rutile group

Graves Montain, Georgia, USA

Crystal system, form and habit Tetragonal, short prismatic, twinning common, often geniculate or lattice-like; usually massive
Hardness 6-6.5
Cleavage Basal and prismatic
Specific gravity 4.23
Colour Reddish-brown to red; yellow to orange or grey to black
Lustre Splendent adamantine
Streak Pale brown to yellowish
Diaphaneity Translucent to transparent
Name From the Latin rutilus, alluding to the colour

Polymorphous with anatase and brookite, rutile is found in a number of different environments. Fine quartz crystals with golden rutile inclusions are used ornamentally. Good quality crystals from European Alpine locations. From pegmatites at Kragerö (Norway); from hydrothermal alpine-type mineral veins; in the Zillertal at Saurüssel (Austria) and in the Binntal, Urserental and Tavetschtal (Switzerland); from Magnet Cove, Arkansas (USA) and elsewhere as needles and grains in sediments and metamorphic rocks and as a detrital mineral in sands and placer deposits in New South Wales (Australia) and Brazil.

Sapphirine

$(Mg,Al)_8(Al,Si)_6O_{20}$

Madagascar

Crystal system, form and habit Triclinic, tabular
Hardness 7.5
Cleavage Indistinct
Specific gravity 3.4-3.5
Colour Pale to greenish blue
Lustre Vitreous
Refractive index 1.71-1.72
Name From its colour

Sapphirine is a mineral of high-temperature metamorphism found in rocks with a high aluminium and low silicon content. It has been found in the pegmatites at Itrongay, Madagascar and at Fiskernaes on the west coast of Greenland. Also found at the Alpe Brasciadega, Val Codera, Sondrio (Italy).

Scapolite
Scapolite group

Marialite: $NaAlSi_3O_8.NaCl$

Meionite: $CaAl_2Si_2O_8.CaCO_3$

Minas Gerais, Brazil; Tanzania (stone)

Crystal system, form and habit Tetragonal, forming prismatic crystals
Hardness 6
Cleavage Poor prismatic

Specific gravity 2.50-2.74
Colour Pink, yellow, purple, colourless
Lustre Vitreous
Refractive index 1.540-1.549
Diaphaneity Transparent to translucent
Other features As scapolite forms part of an isomorphous series between the end members marialite and meionite, constants and colours show wide variation as do the different and attractive fluorescent effects.
Name From the Greek word for shaft, alluding to the crystal habit

Scapolite is found in contact zones and altered basic igneous rocks, also in metamorphic rocks. Fine gem material, pink and violet, some chatoyant, from the gemstone area of Upper Burma; fine yellow citrine-like crystals from Tanzania, the state of Espirito Santo (Brazil) and from Madagascar. From Tremorgio, Ticino (Switzerland).

Scheelite

$CaWO_4$

Korea

Crystal system, form and habit Tetragonal; octahedral or massive

Hardness 4.5-5
Cleavage 3 distinct directions
Specific gravity 5.9-6.3
Colour Colourless to yellow
Lustre Vitreous to adamantine
Refractive index 1.918-1.937
Diaphaneity Translucent to transparent
Other features May show faint didymium lines in the absorption spectrum; brilliant blue-white fluorescence SWUV
Name From Swedish chemist K W Scheele

Found in contact metamorphic deposits, hydrothermal veins, pegmatites and in placer deposits. From Bishop and Atolia, California; orange-brown gem quality crystals from Sonora (Mexico); from Tong Wha (Korea). From the Ramsley mine, Sticklepath, Devon (England); from Bruchgraben, Hollersbachtal (Austria); Tavetsch (Switzerland); Iragna, Ticino (Switzerland); Hunan and Liaoning (China).

Schorl

$NaFe_3^{2+}Al_6(BO_3)_3Si_6O_{18}(OH)_4$

Tourmaline group

Sonora, Mexico

Crystal system, form and habit Trigonal, forming short to long deeply striated prismatic crystals, commonly hemimorphic
Hardness 7.25
Specific gravity 3.10-3.25
Colour Black, brown to bluish-black
Lustre Vitreous
Refractive index 1.65-1.67
Streak Colourless

Found characteristically in granite pegmatites, worldwide. Notably from Woolley Farm, Bovey Tracey, Devon (England). Forms a series with dravite.

Scolecite

$CaAl_2Si_3O_{10}.3H_2O$

Zeolite group

India

Crystal system, form and habit Monoclinic, slender prismatic or fibrous radial masses
Hardness 5
Cleavage Good prismatic
Specific gravity 2.27
Colour Colourless or white
Lustre Vitreous, silky when fibrous
Name From the Greek word for worm as the mineral curls up in the borax bead test

Found mostly in cavities in basalt and related rocks, also from contact zones and schists. Found in the trap rocks of New Jersey and fine crystals come from Rio Grande do Sul (Brazil).

Scorodite

$FeAsO_4.2H_2O$

Zacatecas, Mexico

Crystal system, form and habit Orthorhombic, pyramidal crystals, more commonly as drusy crusts or masses

Hardness 3.5-4
Cleavage Several poorly-developed directions
Specific gravity 3.27
Colour Pale greyish-green, bluish-green, blue or violet, yellowish-brown to brown
Lustre Vitreous to resinous
Refractive index 1.784-1.814
Diaphaneity Transparent to translucent
Other features Soluble in HCl
Name From the Greek word for garlic, referring to the smell when heated

Usually occurs by the oxidation of arsenic-bearing minerals. Large blue crystals from Mexico, in particular El Cobre mine, Concepcion del Oro (Mexico). From Grube Clara, Schwarzwald (Germany); Cetine, Siena and Montevecchio, Sardinia (Italy), and from Ouro Preto (Brazil); also from Carinthia (Austria) and Cornwall (England).

Sepiolite

$Mg_4Si_6O_{15}(OH)_2 \cdot 6H_2O$

Kennack, Cornwall, England

Crystal system, form and habit Orthorhombic, forming fibrous masses
Hardness 2-2.5
Specific gravity About 2
Colour White, grey, yellowish or tinted with blue, green or red
Lustre Dull
Name From the Greek word for cuttlefish, alluding to the mineral's lightness and porosity

Found as an alteration product of serpentine or magnesite and providing the meerschaum used for pipes. Fine nodular masses from Eskehir (Turkey).

Serandite

$Na(Mn^{2+},Ca)_2Si_3O_8(OH)$

Mont St Hilaire, Quebec, Canada

Crystal system, form and habit Triclinic, thick tabular or prismatic, sometimes forming aggregates
Hardness 4.5-5
Cleavage Perfect
Specific gravity 3.32
Colour Rose red to pink
Lustre Vitreous to pearly
Refractive index 1.660-1.688
Diaphaneity Transparent
Name From J-M Serand, West African mineral collector

Found in a carbonatite at Mont St Hilaire, Quebec (Canada) with analcime and other minerals, and from a nepheline syenite from Rouma, Los Islands (Guinea).

Serpentine

Kaolinite-serpentine group

A group of minerals with the general composition $A_3Si_2O_5(OH)$ where A= magnesium, ferrous iron or nickel

Pakistan

Crystal system, form and habit Monoclinic and orthorhombic; forms masses of fibres

Hardness 2.5 (the variety bowenite 4-6)
Cleavage Perfect
Specific gravity 2.44-2.62; bowenite 2.58-2.62
Diaphaneity Translucent to opaque
Other features Yellowish varieties may fluoresce cream-yellow
Name From the Latin word for serpent, alluding to the surface patterning of some serpentine rocks

Formed by the alteration of basic and ultrabasic rocks, bowenite may be dark green to yellowish green or yellow. Williamsite is apple green; Connemara marble is a mixture of lizardite serpentine and carbonate minerals; it shows greenish-white banding. A green serpentine with calcite veins is known as verd-antique. Pseudophite is an aluminous serpentine and is sometimes fashioned. Lizardite from the Lizard, Cornwall (England); a chrome green variety of williamsite from Rock Springs, Maryland (USA); pseudophite from Styria (Austria) and Greece. Antigorite is platy.

Shattuckite

$Cu_5(SiO_3)_4(OH)_2$

Ajo, Arizona, USA

Crystal system, form and habit Orthorhombic, slender prismatic; sometimes as radiating aggregates
Cleavage Very good
Specific gravity 4.1
Colour Blue to dark blue
Lustre Vitreous to silky
Diaphaneity Translucent
Name For the Shattuck Arizona Copper Company mine, Bisbee, Arizona (USA)

Found as an alteration product of other copper minerals at the Shattuck mine, Bisbee, Arizona (USA)

Siderite

$FeCO_3$

Allevard, France

Crystal system, form and habit Trigonal; rhombohedral or scalenohedral
Hardness 3.5-4.5

Cleavage Perfect rhombohedral
Specific gravity 3.96
Colour Yellowish-brown to brown or green
Lustre Vitreous to pearly or silky
Refractive index 1.87-1.63
Streak White
Diaphaneity Transparent to translucent
Other features Some surfaces may show an iridescent tarnish; slowly soluble in cold acid, rapidly in hot
Name From the Greek word for iron

Rarely cut as a dark brown gemstone, siderite is common and well-distributed through the Earth. Economically important deposits occur in bedded sediments with shale or coal seams. Also occurring in hydrothermal metallic veins and in basaltic rocks, in some pegmatites and as a replacement of limestones by iron solutions. Fine crystals from Traversella, Piedmont (Italy) and from Tavetsch, Grisons (Switzerland). Well-crystallized specimens from the Cornish tin veins, particularly from the Great Onslow Consols mine, St Breward, Wheal Maudlin, Lanlivery and the Penlee quarry, St Just (England); from the Virtuous Lady mine, Buckland Monachorum, Devon (England). Found in the silver-lead mines at Coeur d'Alene, Idaho (USA). From pegmatitic-pneumatolytic areas of Ivigtut (Greenland) and from Panasqueira (Portugal); Zhejiang (China). Forms a series with magnesite and with rhodochrosite.

Sillimanite

Al_2SiO_5

Connecticut, USA

usually fibrous massive
Hardness 6.5-7.5
Cleavage Perfect pinacoidal
Specific gravity 3.23-3.27
Colour Colourless, white, grey, crystals pale bluish-grey
Lustre Vitreous to silky
Refractive index 1.654-1.683
Streak Colourless
Diaphaneity Translucent to transparent
Name From American geologist Benjamin Silliman

Crystal system, form and habit Orthorhombic, long prismatic, square cross-section;

Polymorphous with kyanite and andalusite the very fibrous sillimanite has, amazingly, been faceted into gemstones. It is a characteristic mineral of metamorphic rocks such as schists and gneisses. It also occurs in granites. Best gem-quality material comes from Burma or Sri Lanka; from Freiberg, Saxony (East Germany); Bodenmais (Bavaria); Sellrain, Otztal, Tirol (Austria).

Silver

Ag

Houghton County, Michigan, USA

dral crystals, sometimes dodecahedral; also arborescent or as wires or scales; twinning common
Hardness 2.5-3
Specific gravity 10.5
Colour Silvery white often with grey to black tarnish
Lustre Metallic
Other features Malleable and ductile
Name From an Old English word for the metal

Crystal system, form and habit Cubic, as cubic or octahe-

Found in the oxidation zone of ore deposits with other silver minerals; also hydrothermal veins. From many places in the world; notable specimens from Kongsberg (Norway); Freiberg, Aue and Mansfeld (East Germany); Jachymov (Czechoslovakia); Huanchaca (Bolivia); Quincy mine, Hancock, Michigan (USA); from Juangxi (China). Forms a series with gold.

Skutterudite

(Co,Ni,Fe)As₃

Bou Azzer, Morocco

Crystal system, form and habit Cubic, usually massive; rare crystals are cubes or octahedra.
Hardness 5.5-6
Specific gravity 6.1-6.8
Colour Tin white
Lustre Metallic
Name From the Norwegian locality, Skutterud

Found in medium-temperature veins with silver and related cobalt and nickel minerals. Highly cobalt-rich specimens from Bou Azzer (Morocco) form the finest crystals; also from Skutterud and Snarum (Norway); Annaberg and Schneeberg, Saxony (East Germany); Jachymov (Czechoslovakia), Les Chalanches, Dauphiné (France).

Smithsonite

ZnCO₃

Calcite group

Tsumeb, Namibia
Crystal system, form and habit Trigonal; usually botryoidal or stalactitic
Hardness 4-4.5
Cleavage Rhombohedral, often

curved
Specific gravity 4.3-4.4
Colour White to grey; shades of green to blue-green; occasionally approaches the green of jade
Lustre Vitreous, with pearly on cleavage faces
Refractive index 1.848-1.621
Streak White
Diaphaneity Translucent
Other features Effervesces with acids
Name From James Smithson, founder of the Smithsonian Institution, Washington DC (USA)

Smithsonite is found in the oxidized zone of zinc ore deposits. Specimens in various colours occur with the lead and zinc slags at Laurium (Greece), site of Roman silver workings; fine masses of a beautiful green occur at the Kelly mine, Socorro County, New Mexico (USA); Altenberge and Wiesloch (West Germany); Bleiberg (Austria); Tsumeb (Namibia); Monteponi and Iglesias (Sardinia); Broken Hill, New South Wales (Australia); Guangxi (China).

Sodalite $Na_8Al_6Si_6O_{24}Cl_2$

Sodalite group

Ontario, Canada

Crystal system, form and habit Cubic, usually dodecahedral or massive

Hardness 5.5-6
Cleavage Poor dodecahedral
Specific gravity 2.14-2.40
Colour Colourless light to dark blue, reddish or greenish
Lustre Vitreous to greasy
Refractive index 1.483-1.487
Streak Colourless
Diaphaneity Transparent to translucent
Other features May fluoresce yellow to orange LWUV
Name From its composition

Found mainly in nepheline-syenites and related rocks. From Ditro, Transylvania (Romania); Sierra de Monchique (Portugal): from trachytes and basalt, also volcanic ejecta from Somma, Vesuvius (Italy); Rieden, Laacher See, Eifel (West Germany).

Spessartine $Mn_3Al_2(SiO_4)_3$

Garnet group

Little Three mine, California, USA

Crystal system, form and habit Cubic, forming rhombic dodecahedra, icositetrahedra or combinations
Hardness 7-7.5
Specific gravity 3.80-4.25
Colour Pale orange to dark red
Lustre Vitreous
Refractive index 1.8
Diaphaneity Transparent
Name For Spessart, Bavaria

Spessartine is found in granite pegmatites or in gneisses and schists. Fine crystals from the Rutherford mine, Amelia, Virginia and the Ramona mine, San Diego County, California (USA). Also as fine crystals from a rhyolite near Ely, White Pine County, Nevada (USA) and from Norway. Much dark red gem material from pegmatites in Brazil; in galena from Broken Hill, New South Wales (Australia). Forms a series with almandine.

Sphaerocobaltite $CoCO_3$

Calcite group

Katanga, Zaire

Crystal system, form and habit Trigonal; small spherical masses
Hardness 4
Specific gravity 4.13
Colour Rose red
Lustre Vitreous to waxy
Refractive index 1.60-1.85
Other features Alters to black or brown on exposure
Name From Greek word for ball and from the element cobalt

Found in cobalt-nickel veins at Schneeberg, Saxony (East Germany); Boleo, Baja, California (USA); Concepcion del Oro (Mexico).

Sphalerite $(Zn,Fe)S$

Sphalerite group

Santander, Spain

Crystal system, form and habit Cubic, tetrahedral, octahedral-appearing crystals or as masses; commonly twinned
Hardness 3.5-4
Cleavage Perfect dodecahedral
Specific gravity 3.9-4.1
Colour Brown, green, orange to yellow, red, colourless
Lustre Resinous to adamantine
Refractive index 2.369
Streak Pale brown to colourless
Diaphaneity Transparent to opaque
Other features May show

fluorescence (orange) or triboluminescence
Name From the Greek for treacherous or slippery, alluding to the mineral's being mistaken for galena, but giving no lead

Polymorphous with wurtzite and with matraite, sphalerite is also known as zinc blende or blende. It is the commonest zinc mineral and has occasionally been faceted despite its easy cleavage and softness. Commonly associated with galena and other sulphides in limestones, dolomites and other sedimentary rocks. Found also in hydrothermal ore veins. Fine material from Picos de Europa, Santander (Spain); Anneberg and Saxberget (Sweden); Pribram (Czechoslovakia); Mies (Yugoslavia); sedimentary deposits near Meggen, Westphalia and metamorphic deposits at Rammelsberg (West Germany). From Franklin, New Jersey and as minute 'ruby jack' incrustations from Joplin, Missouri (USA). From the Lorano quarry, Carrara marble quarries and from Campione, Grosseto (Italy). Recently clear dark green crystals were found at the Iron Cap mine, Graham County, Arizona (USA). From Hunan and Guanxi (China).

Sphene   CaTiSiO$_5$

Brazil

Crystal system, form and habit Monoclinic, wedge-shaped crystals, often twinned; some-times massive
Hardness 5-5.5
Cleavage Distinct prismatic
Specific gravity 3.45-3.55
Colour Yellow, green, emerald green, brown to black
Lustre Adamantine to resinous
Refractive index 1.843-2.110
Streak White
Diaphaneity Transparent to translucent
Name From the Greek word for wedge

Frequently cut as a gemstone, sphene (titanite) is found in igneous and metamorphic rocks. It is common in nepheline-syenites. Good crystals are characteristic of European Alpine locations and rare emerald-green crystals are known from Baja California (Mexico). Various colours from Burma. Generally tabular crystals from veins in silicate rocks as at Kragerö (Norway); Pfitsch, Tirol (Austria), St Gotthard and Tavetsch (Switzerland). In igneous rocks and crystalline schists common sphene is the rule as in sanidine ejecta from Laacher See, Eifel

(West Germany). Good gem quality material from a pegmatite at Capelinha, Minas Gerais (Brazil). Once from the Tilly Foster mine, Brewster, New York as yellow-brown transparent crystals. Also from Teufelsmühle, Habachtal and Bruchgraben, Hollersbachtal (Austria). Yellow gemmy crystals from the Gardiner complex (Greenland).

Spinel

MgAl$_2$O$_4$

Spinel group

Sri Lanka

Crystal system, form and habit Cubic, usually octahedra, commonly twinned with one half rotated through 1800

Hardness 7.5-8
Specific gravity 3.6
Colour Shades of red, blue, brown to black
Lustre Vitreous
Refractive index 1.718
Streak White
Diaphaneity Transparent to opaque
Other features Red crystals fluoresce red under LWUV
Name From the Latin word for little thorn, alluding to the crystal shape

Spinel is found in metamorphosed limestones. Gem quality crystals (red and blue) from Burma and the gem gravels of Sri Lanka; also from Thailand; Zlatoust, Ural Mountains (USSR). Fine blue crystals from Helena, Montana (USA). Forms a series with gahnite and with hercynite.

Spodumene

LiAlSi$_2$O$_6$

Pyroxene group

Afghanistan

Crystal system, form and habit Monoclinic, flattened prismatic, vertically striated
Hardness 6.5-7.5
Cleavage Perfect prismatic
Specific gravity 3.0-3.2
Colour Colourless, yellow, pink, green, emerald green, violet
Lustre Vitreous
Diaphaneity Transparent to translucent

Spodumene is a characteristic mineral of granite pegmatites. Gem varieties are kunzite, lilac and yellow; emerald-green hiddenite only from the area of Stony Point, Alexander County, North Carolina (USA). Mostly from Brazil, in particular, fine kunzite from the Urupuca mine, Fazenda Anglo, Minas Gerais, but also found in Afghanistan, Pakistan; fine kunzite from Pala, San Diego County, California (USA) and from Madagascar; from Xinjiang (China).

Staurolite $(Fe,Mg,Zn)_2Al_9(Si,Al)_4O_{22}(OH)_2$

Georgia, USA

Crystal system, form and habit Monoclinic, pseudo-orthorhombic characteristic cross-like twins
Hardness 7-7.5
Cleavage Distinct
Specific gravity 3.65-3.83
Colour Dark to yellowish-brown
Lustre Vitreous to resinous
Refractive index 1.739-1.761
Streak Grey
Diaphaneity Translucent to near-transparent
Other features Pleochroism yellowish-red/gold
Name From the Greek word for cross

Staurolite is found in metamorphic rocks including schists and gneisses. Crossed crystals come from Virginia, North Carolina and Georgia (USA). Fine crystals from Monte Campione (Switzerland) found with kyanite; also from the Hohe Tauern (Austria) and the Gorob mine (Namibia).

Stephanite

Ag$_5$SbS$_4$

Saxony, East Germany

Crystal system, form and habit Orthorhombic, usually well-formed crystals, intergrown to look hexagonal on occasion
Hardness 2-2.5
Cleavage 2 poor
Specific gravity 6.2-6.3
Colour Iron black
Lustre Metallic
Name From the mining director and archduke of Austria Victor Stephan

Stephanite is found with other sulphides such as galena and sphalerite and with native silver and the ruby silvers proustite and pyrargyrite. From the Comstock Lode, Nevada (USA) and from the silver-bearing areas of Saxony (East Germany). Also from Bolivia and from Cornwall (England), particularly from Wheal Newton, Harrowberrow, Calstock.

Stibnite

Sb$_2$S$_3$

Nagybanya, Romania

Crystal system, form and habit Orthorhombic, stout to slender prisms, often in aggregates

Hardness 2
Cleavage Perfect side pinacoidal
Specific gravity 4.63
Colour Lead to steel-grey
Lustre Metallic, splendent on cleavage surfaces
Refractive index 3.19-4.30
Streak Lead to steel grey
Other features Slightly sectile; soluble in HCl; blackish tarnish, sometimes iridescent
Name From a Greek word referring to stibnite's use as an eye adornment

Stibnite is the most important ore of antimony and is formed in low-temperature hydrothermal veins and in hot springs. Fine crystal groups come from the mines at Ichinokawa, Shikoku (Japan); good crystals also from limestones at Pereta, Tuscany (Italy) and in central France, at Lubilhac, Haute-Loire. It is also found at Wolfsburg, Harz (West Germany) and at Felsobanya (Romania), where it occurs as radiating aggregates with barite; also from Lesnica (Yugoslavia). From Wheal Boys, St Endellion, Cornwall (England).

Stichtite

$Mg_6Cr_2(CO_3)(OH)_{16}.4H_2O$

Tasmania, Australia
Crystal system, form and

habit Trigonal, massive, foliated
Hardness 1.5-2.5
Cleavage Perfect
Specific gravity 2.16-2.22
Colour White to lilac
Lustre Pearly to waxy; feels greasy
Refractive index 1.54-1.51
Other features Forms flexible laminae; Cr absorption spectrum
Name From Robert Sticht, Tasmanian mining manager

Stichtite is found associated with chromite in serpentine rocks. Massive material cut into ornaments; best specimens from Tasmania and South Africa but also found at Black Lake, Quebec (Canada).

Stilbite

$NaCa_2Al_5Si_{13}O_{36}.14H_2O$

Zeolite group

New Jersey, USA
Crystal system, form and habit Monoclinic and triclinic, cruciform penetration twins or

masses
Hardness 3.5-4
Cleavage Perfect
Specific gravity 2.09-2.2
Colour White, grey, yellowish, orange, pink, light brown
Lustre Vitreous, pearly on cleavage
Streak Colourless
Diaphaneity Transparent to translucent
Name From the Greek for to shine, alluding to the cleavage lustre

Found in cavities in basalt, andesite and related volcanic rocks, cavities in granite pegmatites and in some hot spring deposits. From Cowlitz County, Washington (USA); traprocks of New

Jersey, especially from Paterson. Bright orange crystals from
Kilpatrick (Scotland) and Great Notch, New Jersey (USA),
also from Brazil and India.

Stolzite

$PbWO_4$

Broken Hill, Australia

Crystal system, form and habit Tetragonal, usually
dipyramidal; faces striated
Hardness 2.5-3
Cleavage Indistinct
Specific gravity 7.9-8.3
Colour Red to reddish-brown or yellow
Lustre Resinous to sub-adamantine
Refractive index 2.26-2.18
Streak Colourless
Other features Soluble in HCl
Name From Dr Stolz of Teplitz (Czechoslovakia)

Dimorphous with raspite, stolzite is found with other lead minerals in the oxidized zone of deposits containing tungsten minerals. Found with cerussite at the Force Craig mine, Keswick,
Cumbria (England); with pyromorphite at the Wheatley mine,
Chester, Pennsylvania (USA).

Strontianite

$SrCO_3$

Aragonite group

Westphalia, West Germany

Crystal system, form and habit Orthorhombic, long to
short prismatic, pseudohexagonal
Hardness 3.5
Cleavage 1 good, 1 poor
Specific gravity 3.76
Colour Colourless, grey, yellow or greenish twinning very com-
mon
Lustre Vitreous to resinous on uneven fracture surfaces
Refractive index 1.51-1.67
Diaphaneity Transparent to translucent
Other features Fluorescent and phosphorescent in UV, some-
times thermoluminescent. Solu-ble in dilute HCl
Name From Scottish location

Usually found in veins in limestone with barite, celestine and calcite. It is also found as geodes or concretions in limestones and clays. Well-shaped crystals occur in the region of Hamm and Munster, particularly at Drensteinfurt, Ascheberg and Ahlen, Westphalia (West Germany). Strontianite is also found at the St Andreasberg mines, Harz (West Germany) and in Scotland (the original source) at Strontian, Argyllshire, where it occurs with barite, calcite and galena in veins in a gneiss. It occurs in the calcite cap rock of salt domes in Texas and Louisiana (USA), bordering the Gulf, where celestine is an accompanying mineral.

Sulphur S

Sicily

Crystal system, form and habit Orthorhombic, thick tabular or dipyramidal

Hardness 1.5-2.5
Cleavage Imperfect basal, prismatic and pyramidal
Specific gravity 2.07
Colour Sulphur to honey-yellow
Lustre Resinous to greasy
Refractive index 1.95-2.25
Streak White
Other features Brittle to imperfectly sectile; heat sensitive and easily melts
Name From a Latin word for the element

Sulphur may be formed by volcanic activity, forming from the gases given off at fumaroles or from the action of acid water on metallic sulphides. It is a frequent product of mine fires through the heating of pyrite. Easily the finest crystals known occur at Agrigento in Sicily where there are very large sulphur deposits. Fine crystals can also be found at Perticara, Romagna (Italy). Very large sulphur beds are found at various places in the United States, particularly in Texas and Louisiana; good crystals from Steamboat Springs, Nevada. Bright yellow transparent crystals from Laurium (Greece); Grube Machow, Tarnobrzeg (Poland); from Xinjiang (China).

Susannite

$Pb_4(SO_4)(CO_3)_2(OH)_2$

Leadhills, Scotland

Crystal system, form and habit Trigonal; rhombohedral crystals
Colour Colourless to greenish
Name From the Scottish mine

Susannite is dimorphous with leadhillite and was first reported from the Susanna mine, Leadhills (Scotland). Also reported from the Mammoth mine, Tiger, Arizona (USA), from Moldawa (Hungary) and from Nertschinsk (Siberia).

Sylvanite

$(Au,Ag)_2Te_4$

Transylvania, Romania

habit Monoclinic, striated prisms, often twinned; also as masses
Hardness 2.5
Cleavage Side pinacoidal
Specific gravity 8.2
Colour Pale brass-yellow to silver-white
Lustre Metallic
Name From Transylvania (Romania) where the mineral was first found
Crystal system, form and

Calaverite becomes sylvanite when 13.4% of the gold is replaced by silver. Important gold ore from Kalgoorlie (Australia) and Cripple Creek, Colorado and Calaveras County, California (USA).

Sylvite

KCl

Germany

Crystal system, form and

habit Cubic, cubes or masses
Hardness 2
Cleavage Perfect Cubic
Specific gravity 1.993
Colour White, grey, bluish, red-dish from hematite inclusions
Lustre Vitreous
Diaphaneity Transparent
Other features Soluble in water; tastes more bitter than halite
Name From the old chemical name for the substance

Found as sedimentary deposits with halite and gypsum. From Mount Etna and Vesuvius (Italy) as a sublimation product; also from the Permian basin of south eastern New Mexico (USA), particularly from Carlsbad; large deposits in north Germany (Galicia) and in the Barcelona area, Catalonia (Spain).

Taaffeite

$Mg_3Al_8BeO_{16}$

Sri Lanka

Crystal system, form and habit Hexagonal, small worn crystals
Hardness 8-8.5
Specific gravity 3.6
Colour Pinkish-lilac
Lustre Vitreous
Refractive index 1.717-1.724
Diaphaneity Transparent
Name From Count Taaffe, dis-coverer of the mineral in faceted form

From alluvial gravels in Sri Lanka.

Talc

$Mg_3Si_4O_{10}(OH)_2$

Hoosac Tunnel, Massachusetts, USA

Crystal system, form and habit Monoclinic and triclinic, thin tabular crystals; usually fine grained masses
Hardness 1
Cleavage Micaceous
Specific gravity 2.58-2.83
Colour Pale to dark green, white, grey, brownish
Lustre Greasy to dull
Streak White
Diaphaneity Translucent to opaque
Other features Greasy feel
Name Perhaps from the Arabic word talq

Found widespread as a secondary mineral formed by the hydrothermal alteration of ultrabasic rocks or the thermal metamorphism of siliceous dolomites. Many locations worldwide. Some material used for carving (soapstone). Notably from the Zillertal, Tirol (Austria); Hospental (Switzerland), Zoblitz, Saxony (East Germany); from Liaoning (China).

Tennantite

$(Cu,Fe)_{12}As_4S_{13}$

Tsumeb, Namibia

Crystal system, form and habit Cubic, cubic habit or massive
Hardness 3-4.5
Specific gravity 4.6-5.1
Colour Grey to iron-black
Lustre Metallic
Other features May show red in thin splinters
Name From the English chemist Smithson Tennant

Tennantite forms a series with tetrahedrite which is softer and more distinctly crystallized. Fine crystals from Bingham Canyon, Utah (USA) and from Schwaz and Brixlegg, Tirol (Austria); Freiberg, Saxony (East Germany); Príbram (Czechoslovakia). Usually formed hydrothermally though occasionally found in pegmatites or pneumatolytic deposits. From Lengenbach, Binntal (Switzerland).

Tetrahedrite

(Cu,Fe)$_{12}$Sb$_4$S$_{13}$

Tetrahedrite group

Longfellow mine, Colorado, USA

Crystal system, form and

habit Cubic, tetrahedral crystals, penetration twinning common
Hardness 3-4.5
Specific gravity 4.6-5.1
Colour Steel grey to iron black
Lustre Metallic
Streak Black to brown to dark red
Other features Deep red in thin sections
Name From its crystal form

Found in low to medium temperature hydrothermal ore veins associated with sulphides, carbonates, quartz and fluorite. Fine crystals from Bingham, Salt Lake County, Utah (USA); Morococha (Peru); Czechoslovakia; England; Campione, Grosseto (Italy); Grube Schone Aussicht, Burback, Siegerland (West Germany).

Thenardite

Na$_2$SO$_4$

Soda Lake, California, USA

Crystal system, form and habit Orthorhombic forming intergrown clusters

Hardness 2.5-3
Cleavage Good basal
Specific gravity 2.7
Colour Colourless to light yellow or brown
Lustre Glassy
Diaphaneity Transparent to translucent
Other features Soluble in water; salty taste; weak yellow-green luminescence and phosphorescence LWUV
Name From the French chemist L J Thenard

Formed by evaporation of salt lakes, as in Searles Lake, California (USA); also from Chile, Spain, Siberia; Xinjiang (China).

Thomsonite

$NaCa_2Al_5Si_5O_{20}.6H_2O$

Zeolite group

Michigan, New Mexico, USA

Crystal system, form and

habit Orthorhombic, prismatic or acicular crystals; usually radiating or lamellar aggregates
Hardness 5-5.5
Cleavage Perfect
Specific gravity 2.25-2.40
Colour Colourless, white, yellowish, pink or greenish
Lustre Vitreous to pearly
Streak Colourless
Name From the Scottish chemist Thomas Thomson

Found in amygdules in basalt and related igneous rocks, also in schists. From the traprocks of New Jersey; agate-like pebbles from Grand Marais, Cook County, Minnesota (USA); from Vesuvius (Italy); near Eisenach (West Germany) and Waltsch, Bohemia (Czechoslovakia).

Tincalconite

$Na_2B_4O_5(OH)_4.3H_2O$

Boron, California, USA

Crystal system, form and habit Trigonal, occurring as a fine-grained powder
Colour White
Diaphaneity Opaque
Name From a Sanskrit word for borax and a Greek word for powder. This refers to the formation of the mineral from the decomposition of borax

From Searles Lake and Boron, California (USA).

Topaz

$Al_2(F,OH)_2SiO_4$

Gilgit, Pakistan

Crystal system, form and habit Orthorhombic, prismatic

well-developed crystals
Hardness 8
Cleavage Perfect basal
Specific gravity 3.53
Colour Brown, yellow, orange-red, blue, pink, colourless
Lustre Vitreous
Refractive index 1.62-1.64
Streak Colourless
Diaphaneity Transparent
Name From Topazion, an island in the Red Sea

Topaz is found in pegmatites and most of the world's gem material comes from various mines in Minas Gerais (Brazil), the town of Ouro Preto being a centre for the mining; particularly important crystals come from a belt west of the town, including the Saramenha, Dom Bosco and Rodrigo Silva mines. Crystals also from Utah (USA); Sri Lanka; fine blue crystals from Zimbabwe and fine dark pink crystals from Katlang (Pakistan). Also from Alabaschka, Mursinsk, Urals (USSR) and fine well-developed colourless crystals from the Nigerian tin mining area. From the little three mine, Ramona, California; Stocker Alm, Untersulzbachtal, Hohe Tauern (Aus-(Austria); Schneckenstein, Auerbach, Saxony, (East Germany); Mourne Mountains (Northern Ireland); Klein Spitzkopje (Namibia); Drammen (Norway), Nai Monggol Autonomous Region (China).

Torbernite

$Cu(UO_2)(PO_4)_2.8\text{-}12\ H_2O$

Katanga, Zaire

Crystal system, form and

habit Tetragonal, usually forming thin square plates or small bipyramids; micaceous flakes
Hardness 2-2.5
Cleavage Perfect basal and good frontal
Specific gravity 3.2-3.6
Colour Emerald green to yellow-ish-green
Lustre Pearly or vitreous
Name From the Swedish mineralogist Torbern Olaf Bergman

Green micaceous plates are found in pegmatites; fine crystals from Gunnislake, Cornwall (England) and from Mount Painter (Australia); magnificent green crystals from Shaba province (Zaire) and from the uranium-vanadium deposit of Mounana (Gabon).

Tremolite
$Ca_2(Mg,Fe^{2+})_5Si_8O_{22}(OH)_2$

Amphibole group

Balmat, New York, USA

Crystal system, form and habit Monoclinic, long bladed, crystals; usually fibrous aggregates or masses.
Hardness 5-6
Cleavage Perfect prismatic
Specific gravity 2.9-3.2
Colour Colourless, grey, pale greenish, pink, brown
Lustre Vitreous
Diaphaneity Transparent to translucent
Other features May fluoresce
Name From the Tremola valley, St Gotthard, Switzerland

Found in contact and regionally metamorphosed dolomites, magnesian limestone and some ultrabasic rocks. The pink transparent variety hexagonite occurs only at Edwards, New York (USA). Fine green crystals from Passo Cadonighino, Ticino (Switzerland). Forms a series with actinolite and ferroactiolite.

Triphylite
$LiFePO_4$

Smith mine, New Hampshire, USA

Crystal system, form and habit Orthorhombic, massive
Hardness 4.5-5.0
Cleavage 1 fair, 2 imperfect
Colour Grey blue to blue green
Diaphaneity Transparent to translucent
Name From the Greek for three and family, alluding to its optical nature

Forms isomorphous series with lithiophilite which is pink to greenish-brown with the composition $LiMnPO_4$. Good crystals of triphylite from Chandler's Mill, Newport, New Hampshire (USA) and Pala, San Diego County, California. From Rajasthan (India); Mangualde (Portugal); Rio Grande do Norte (Brazil).

Tungstite $WO_3.H_2O$

Bolivia

Crystal system, form and habit Orthorhombic, small scaly crystals
Hardness 2.5
Cleavage 2, but hard to detect
Specific gravity 5.5
Colour Yellow-earth colour
Streak Powdery yellow
Name From its composition

Occurs as a secondary mineral from the alteration of tungsten minerals. Found with tungsten ores in Cornwall (England) and Bolivia. Fine specimens from wolframite mines at Ciudad Rodrigo (Spain).

Turquoise $CuAl_6(PO_4)_4(OH)_8.4H_2O$

Australia

Crystal system, form and habit Triclinic, crystals rare, short prismatic; usually massive or stalactitic
Hardness 5-6
Specific gravity 2.6-2.8
Colour Pale to sky blue or bluish-green
Lustre Waxy lustre
Refractive index 1.61-1.65
Name From a French word for Turkish

Found as a secondary mineral formed by the action of surface waters on aluminous rocks. Finest gem quality material from Nishapur (Iran), for example the Abdurrezzagi mine, Maden; less good quality material from south-west USA. Also from

Australia and Chile; small crystals from Lynch, Virginia (USA); Los Cerillos Mountains, New Mexico (USA). From West Phoenix mine, Linkinhorne, Cornwall (England).

Ulexite

$NaCaB_5O_6(OH)_6.5H_2O$

Boron, California, USA

Crystal system, form and habit Triclinic, crystals acicular; commonly as nodules or compacted fibrous tufted masses
Hardness 2.5
Cleavage Perfect
Specific gravity 1.95
Colour Colourless
Lustre Vitreous or silky (aggregates white)
Diaphaneity Translucent to opaque
Other features Slightly soluble in hot water
Name From the German chemist G L Ulex

Found in playa deposits and in arid regions in California (USA) and elsewhere. 'Television stone' allows print to be read along the direction of the fibres.

Uraninite

UO_2

New Hampshire, USA

Crystal system, form and habit Cubic, cubes or octahedra; massive with banded radial fibrous structure
Hardness 5-6
Cleavage Octahedral
Specific gravity 7.5-10
Colour Black to brownish black
Lustre Submetallic lustre
Diaphaneity Opaque
Name From its composition

Uraninite or pitchblende is radioactive and the chief ore of uranium. Mainly from hydrothermal vein deposits, bedded sedimentary rocks and pegmatites. Large crystals from the Bancroft area of Ontario (Canada); from the pegmatites of the Black Hills, South Dakota (USA). A good deal of material comes from the Katanga district of Zaire and from Rum Jungle,

Northern Territory (Australia); Schneeberg and Annaberg, Saxony (East Germany).

Uvarovite

$Ca_3Cr_2(SiO_4)_3$

Garnet group

Outokumpu, Finland

Crystal system, form and

habit Cubic, forming rhombic dodecahedra, icositetrahedra or combinations
Hardness 6.5-7
Specific gravity 3.4-3.8
Colour Emerald green
Lustre Vitreous
Refractive index 1.86
Streak White
Name From Count S S Uvarov, a Russian nobleman

Found with chromite in serpentine and in metamorphosed limestones. Fine crystals from Outokumpu (Finland) and from Bisersk (USSR); Val Malenco (Italy). Forms a series with grossular.

Uvite

$(Ca,Na)(Mg,Fe^{2+})_3Al_5Mg(BO_3)_3Si_6O_{18}(OH,F)_4$

Tourmaline group

Gouverneur, New York, USA

Crystal system, form and habit Trigonal, prismatic, vertically striated
Hardness 7-7.5
Specific gravity 3.04
Colour Brown, red, blue, green, yellow, colourless
Lustre Vitreous
Refractive index 1.64-1.67
Diaphaneity Transparent to translucent
Name From the province of Uva (Sri Lanka)

Found as a characteristic mineral of metamorphosed limestones with many occurrences worldwide.

Vanadinite

$Pb_5(VO_4)_3Cl$

Apatite group

Arizona, USA

Crystal system, form and habit Hexagonal, short to long prismatic

Hardness 2.75-3
Specific gravity 6.88
Colour Orange red
Lustre Sub-resinous to sub-adamantine
Refractive index 2.3-2.4
Streak White or yellowish
Diaphaneity Transparent to translucent
Other features Easily soluble in HNO_3
Name From its composition

Found in the oxidized zone of lead deposits. Found at Wanlockhead (Scotland) with smithsonite and large crystals at Djebel Mahseur (Morocco); at Beresovsk, Urals (USSR) and very fine crystals from the Old Yuma and Red Cloud mines in Arizona (USA); from mines in New Mexico (USA). Associated minerals include pyromorphite, mimetite, wulfenite and cerussite; also from Tsumeb (Namibia); Bleiberg, Carinthia (Austria); Mies (Yugoslavia); Los Lamentos (Mexico); Mibladen (Morocco). Recently from the J C Holmes claim, Santa Cruz County and the Hamburg mine, Yuma county, Arizona (USA). From the Monti Livornesi, Tuscany (Italy); Gansu (China).

Variscite

$Al(PO_4).2H_2O$

Variscite group

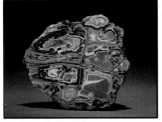

Lewiston, Utah, USA

Crystal system, form and habit Orthorhombic, variscite

massive forming thin crusts of small pyramidal crystals, strengite forming small crystals and botryoidal crusts
Hardness 3.5-4.5
Specific gravity 2.2-2.8
Colour Porcellanous variscite is light or emerald-green, strengite pink to amethyst colour
Name From the Latin Variscia, the name for the Voigtland area of Germany

Derived from the breakdown of minerals in surrounding rock; variscite found in veins. Rounded nodules from Fairfield, Utah, and Lucin, Utah (USA); fine green translucent nodules from Reust, Ronneburg, Vogtland, (East Germany). Variscite forms a series with the iron-aluminium phosphate strengite which is found in iron mines as a late mineral in crusts and small crystals. The best crystals come from a pegmatite at Pleystein (West Germany); also from an altered triphylite at Bull Moose mine, Custer, South Dakota (USA). Radiating pink rosettes found in a phosphate-bearing pegmatite in Rio Grande do Norte (Brazil).

Vesuvianite $Ca_{10}Mg_2Al_4(SiO_4)_5(Si_2O_7)_2(OH)_4$

Asbestos, Quebec, Canada

Crystal system, form and habit Tetragonal, euhedral prismatic crystals; californite is massive and a mixture of vesuvianite and grossular garnet
Hardness 6-7
Cleavage Poor prismatic
Specific gravity 3.32-3.47 (californite 3.25-3.32)
Colour Yellow, brown, reddish; green to dark greenish-brown
Refractive index 1.712-1.721
Diaphaneity Transparent to translucent
Name From Mount Vesuvius, Italy

Vesuvianite (alternatively named idocrase) is a characteristic mineral of serpentinites and contact metamorphic deposits. Fine chrome green and violet material from Asbestos, Quebec (Canada) and also from Quetta (Pakistan). Brown clear crystals from Kenya. Californite from California (USA). The mineral is also found at Pfitsch, Tirol (Austria); Zermatt (Switzerland); Canzocoli and Predazzo, Fassa Valley and Monte Somma (Italy); Italian Mountain, Colorado (USA).

Vivianite

$Fe_3(PO_4)_2.8H_2O$

Vivianite group

Bolivia

Crystal system, form and habit Monoclinic, usually prismatic, flattened and blade-like
Hardness 1.5-2

Cleavage Perfect micaceous
Specific gravity 2.68
Colour Colourless altering to greenish-blue on exposure
Lustre Vitreous, pearly on cleavage surfaces
Refractive index 1.57-1.62
Streak Colourless altering to dark brown
Other features Easily soluble in acids; flexible laminae
Name From J G Vivian, English mineralogist

Vivianite occurs as a secondary mineral in the gossan of metallic ore deposits. Large (over 4in/10cm) are found in the tin veins at Llallagua (Bolivia) and the mineral is also found in the tin veins at St Agnes, Cornwall (England) and in the pegmatites in the Hagendorf area of Bavaria (West Germany). Fine specimens are found at Leadville, Lake County, Colorado (USA); from Cerro de Pasco (Peru); Trepca (Yugoslavia).

Wavellite

$Al_3(PO_4)_2(OH,F)_3.5H_2O$

Hot Springs, Arkansas, USA

Crystal system, form and habit Orthorhombic, acicular radiating aggregates

Hardness 3.25-4
Cleavage Perfect dome and side pinacoid
Specific gravity 2.36
Colour White, greenish-white or green, yellow, yellowish-brown
Lustre Vitreous to pearly
Streak White
Diaphaneity Transparent to translucent
Name From the English physician William Wavell who discovered the mineral

Found as a secondary mineral in hydrothermal veins, in phosphate rocks and some aluminous metamorphic rocks. Fine specimens from Dug Hill, Avant, Garland County, Hot Spring and Montgomery Counties, Arkansas (USA). From St Austell, Cornwall, Barnstaple and High Down quarry, Filleigh, South Molton, Devon (England). From Langenstriegis and Giessen (East Germany); Llallagua (Bolivia); Ouro Preto (Brazil).

Whewellite

$CaC_2O_4.H_2O$

Dresden, East Germany

Crystal system, form and habit Monoclinic, coarse crystalline masses; twins common, crystals equant or short prismatic
Hardness 2.5-3
Cleavage Very good
Specific gravity 2.21-2.23
Colour Colourless, white, yellowish to brown
Lustre Vitreous to pearly
Name From William Whewell, English scientist

Found as large crystals in a coal seam near Burgk, Dresden (East Germany). Fine crystals on yellow calcite in septarian concretions along the Cheyenne River, Meade County, South Dakota (USA).

Willemite

Zn_2SiO_4

Franklin, New Jersey, USA

Crystal system, form and habit Trigonal, prismatic or rhombohedral

Hardness 5.5
Cleavage Poor basal
Specific gravity 3.9-4.1
Colour Usually green
Lustre Vitreous to resinous
Refractive index 1.69-1.71
Diaphaneity Transparent to translucent
Other features Intense green fluorescence SWUV sometimes with phosphorescence; triboluminescent
Name From King William I of the Netherlands

Willemite is found in zinc ore bodies or Zn-bearing metamorphic deposits. Green stubby crystals found at Franklin and

Sterling Hill, New Jersey. Blue transparent crystals from nepheline syenites at Mont St Hilaire, Quebec (Canada).

Witherite

BaCO$_3$

Aragonite group

Hardin County, Illinois, USA

Crystal system, form and habit Orthorhombic; twinning gives pseudohexagonal dipyramids; masses common
Hardness 3-3.5

Cleavage Distinct in one direction, poor in another
Specific gravity 4.29
Colour Colourless to pale yellow, brown or green
Lustre Vitreous, resinous on fracture surfaces
Refractive index 1.529-1.677
Streak White
Diaphaneity Translucent
Other features Green, blue or yellow fluorescence SWUV shown by some English material; soluble in HCl
Name From William Withering, English physician

An important source of barium, witherite occurs in low-temperature hydrothermal veins associated with galena and barite. Deposits in the north-east of England are economically important, or were in past times; locations at Fallowfield and Alston Moor are still visited by collectors. Radial aggregates are found at the Tsubaki silver mine (Japan) and large crystals come from Rosiclare, Illinois (USA); also from Leogang and Peggau (Austria).

Wolframite

(Fe,Mn)WO$_4$

Part of hubnerite-ferberite series

Panasqueira, Portugal

Crystal system, form and habit Monoclinic, forming black blades usually embedded in white vein quartz with perfect cleavage on the fracture face
Hardness 4-4.5
Cleavage Perfect side pinacoidal
Specific gravity 7.1-7.5
Colour Black to red-brown
Lustre Submetallic

Fine specimens from Panasqueira (Portugal); Tong Wha (Korea); St Michael's Mount, Cornwall (England); Guangdong (China).

Wollastonite

$CaSiO_3$

Sunnyside mine, Santa Fe, New Mexico, USA

Crystal system, form and habit Triclinic, tabular crystals; usually fibrous masses commonly twinned.

Hardness 4.5-5
Cleavage Perfect pinacoidal
Specific gravity 2.87-3.09
Colour White to greyish, colourless or very pale green
Lustre Vitreous to pearly
Diaphaneity Translucent
Other features Some yellow or orange fluorescence LWUV
Name From the English mineralogist W H Wollaston

A mineral from metamorphosed limestones, most material from Franklin, New Jersey (USA).

Wulfenite

$PbMoO_4$

Rowley mine, Theba, Arizona, USA

Crystal system, form and habit Tetragonal, usually square tabular

Hardness 2.75-3
Cleavage Good pyramidal
Specific gravity 6.5-7
Colour Orange to yellow or bright red
Lustre Resinous to adamantine
Refractive index 2.40-2.28
Streak White
Diaphaneity Transparent to translucent
Other features Soluble in conconcentrated H_2SO_4
Name From the Austrian mineralogist F X Wulfen

Found in the oxidized zones of lead and molybdenum deposits. Fine crystals from Pribram (Czechoslovakia) and from the Red Cloud mine, Yuma County, the Rowley mine, Painted Rock Mountain and from the Silver Bill mine, Gleeson, Arizona

(USA). From Bleiberg, Carinthia (Austria); Mies (Yugoslavia); the Bwlch-Glas mine (Wales); Laurium (Greece); Montevecchio (Sardinia). Also from Chah-Karbose (Iran); Los Lamentos, Chihuahua and from the San Francisco mine, Sonora (Mexico) – this deposit providing thin yellow plates with orange mimetite. From Guansu province (China); small bright yellow crystals from the Whim Well mine, Whim Creek gold field (Australia). Fine translucent micromounts from the Loudville lead mine, Massachusetts (USA).

Xenotime

YPO$_4$

New York, USA

Crystal system, form and habit Tetragonal, short to long prismatic resembling zircon

Hardness 4-5
Cleavage Complete
Specific gravity 4.4-5.1
Colour Yellowish-brown to reddish-brown
Lustre Vitreous to resinous
Refractive index 1.72-1.81
Streak Pale brown yellowish or reddish
Name From Greek words referring to the yttrium having been mistaken for a new element

Xenotime is found as an accessory mineral in acid and alkaline igneous rocks with larger crystals coming from pegmatites. It can be found in Alpine-type veins. It is fairly common in the granite pegmatites of southern Norway and it is also found on Mt Fiba, Ticino and in the Binnental, Valais and Tavetschstal, Grisons (Switzerland). It is found with fluocerite in the Pikes Peak district, Colorado (USA); recently found in the Rauris and Untersulzbachtal (Austria) and from the Bosco pegmatite, Val Vigezzo, Novara (Italy).

Zincite

(Zn,Mn)O

Franklin, New Jersey, USA

Crystal system, form and habit Hexagonal, hemimorphic bipyramidal; often twinned

Hardness 4
Cleavage Perfect prismatic; basal parting
Specific gravity 5.66
Colour Orange to deep red
Lustre Sub-adamantine
Refractive index 2.01-2.02
Streak Orange-yellow
Diaphaneity Translucent to transparent
Other features Red colour from Mn, some material transparent
Name From the composition

Zincite is found in any quantity only at the famous locations of Franklin and Sterling Hill, New Jersey (USA). A very small amount of this has been faceted to form very rare cut stones. Zincite occurs in the granular ore, the crystals being found in the calcite veins which cut the main ore body.

Zircon

ZrSiO$_4$

Renfrew, Ontario, Canada; Sri Lanka (stones)

Crystal system, form and habit Tetragonal, prismatic crys-

tals with pyramidal terminations
Hardness 7.5
Cleavage Poor
Specific gravity 4.6-4.7
Colour Colourless, red, brown, green, yellow
Lustre Vitreous to subadamantine
Refractive index 1.92-2.01
Diaphaneity Transparent to translucent
Other features Often fluoresces yellow-orange
Name From the Arabic Zarqun

Zircon is most commonly found in granites. Best gem quality material from Thailand, Cambodia and neighbouring countries. Some Sri Lanka material is metamict – it has virtually lost its crystalline structure. Most metamict crystals are green or brown. Orange crystals from New South Wales (Australia) and Nigeria; also from Kragero (Norway); Miask, Ural Mountains

(USSR); from Alpine-type veins at Pfitsch, Tirol (Austria). From Orissa (India); Lazio (Italy); Montevecchio, Sardinia (Italy); from the granites of the Nanling Mountains (China).

Zoisite

$Ca_2Al_3(SiO_4)_3(OH)$

Epidote group

Arusha, Tanzania

Crystal system, form and habit Orthorhombic, prismatic, deeply striated vertically
Hardness 6.5-7
Specific gravity 3.35
Colour Green, blue, pink
Lustre Vitreous
Refractive index 1.68-1.72
Diaphaneity Transparent to translucent
Other features Strongly pleochroic
Name From Sigmund Zois, Austrian scholar

Found in regionally metamorphosed rocks such as calcareous schists and shales. Fine blue transparent crystals from Arusha (Tanzania) are known as tanzanite and opaque pink crystals from Greenland as thulite. Many other occurrences.

Museums

Many museums have mineral collections but the standard of curation varies, many local museums having to rely on part-time staff to keep open. While museums associated with particular mines are often very comprehensive, larger collections may be inadequately or incorrectly labelled and it is always better to start with major national collections when beginning the study of minerals. There are very few great collections whose standards can be relied upon and I would suggest that the following institutions should be visited in the first instance, geography permitting:

Natural History Museum, London, England

National Museum of Natural History, Smithsonian Institution, Washington DC, USA

American Museum of Natural History, Central Park, New York, USA

Royal Ontario Museum, Toronto, Canada

A E Fersman Mineralogical Museum, Leninsky Prospekt, Moscow, USSR

Glossary

Acicular Sharp, needle-like crystals

Amorphous Opposite of crystalline. Amorphous substances lack a regular internal atomic structure. Opal and glass are examples

Anion A negatively-charged ion

Anisotropic Crystals within which light travels at different velocities in different directions

Asterism A star-like effect seen usually by reflected light on the top of cabochon-cut gemstones and caused by oriented crystals of another mineral

Birefringence See Double refraction

Cabochon A gemstone cut without facets in a rounded and domed shape with a flat base

Cation A positively-charged ion

Chatoyancy Seen in some cabochon-cut gemstones in which a bright line of light traverses the long direction and is seen against a dark background

Cleavage A direction of atomic weakness seen only in crystals and along which a crystal may easily break

Complex ion Sometimes known as radicals, complex ions consist of sub-groups of atoms bonded together strongly as in many silicates

Covalent bonding Where two or more atoms share their electrons

Density The mass per unit volume of a substance

Double refraction In crystals other than those of the cubic system a ray of incident light is split into two on entering, each ray travelling through the crystal at a different velocity

Efflorescence Some minerals form a fluffy deposit of minute crystals on rocks and mine equipment

Enantiomorphous Crystals with left- or right-handed forms, each the mirror image of the other. Quartz is the best example

Euhedral Crystals showing well-developed faces

Fluorescence The emission of radiation (usually visible light) when a substance is irradiated by higher-energy radiation such as ultra-violet 'light'

Fracture Breakage not along a crystallographic direction

Fumarole A vent from which gases are emitted and characteristic of volcanic activity

Geode A cavity in a rock within which crystals grow towards the centre

Hand specimen A mineral large enough to be seen without magnification

Hopper crystal Hollowed-out crystals formed when edges grow in preference to faces

Hydrothermal processes Formation of minerals from hot, mineralized watery solutions

Inclusions Solid, liquid or gaseous material found inside a mineral

Interfacial angle The angle between adjacent faces on a crystal, measured from the angle between perpendiculars dropped to both faces

Ion An atom with an electrical charge

Ionic bonding Where two atoms bond together by transferring electrons from one to the other

Isomorphous Having the same crystal structure as another mineral, but different chemical composition

Isomorphous series Two or more minerals may show physical and chemical variation along a smooth curve

Isotropic Crystals in which light travels at the same velocity regardless of direction. Amorphous substances and crystals of the cubic system are isotropic

Lamellae Thin, leaf- or page-like mineral layers caused by repeated twinning

Lattice The three-dimensional and regularly repeating atomic arrangement of a crystal, each point in it having identical surroundings

Lustre The nature of a mineral surface from which light is reflected

Matrix The rock or other mineral in which a specimen is embedded

Metamorphism The alteration of existing rocks and their minerals by later geological activity

Phosphorescence The continuation of fluorescence after the activating radiation is turned off

Pleochroism Showing different colours in different directions

Polarized light Light which vibrates in one direction only, parallel to the direction of travel

Polymorph A substance displaying several distinct forms each having the same chemical composition

Pseudomorph A mineral taking on the shape of a previously existing mineral or organic substance is said to be pseudomorphous after that substance, e.g. opalized wood or shell

Refraction The deviation of a ray of light from its path on entering a different transparent medium

Space group One of 230 different ways in which atoms can be arranged in a homogeneous way in an actual or possible crystal structure

Specific gravity The ratio of the density of a mineral to the density of an equal volume of pure water

Streak The colour shown by the powder of a mineral when it is drawn over unglazed porcelain

Unit cell The basic unit of pattern in a crystal; the smallest grouping of atoms which, when repeated in all directions, makes up the complete crystal

Valency The number of electrons an atom must gain or lose to attain the configuration of the most similar inert gas

Zeolites A large family of hydrous alumino-silicates with an easy and reversible loss of their water of hydration

Bibliography

Dana, J. D., *System of Mineralogy*, New York, 1892 &
1944-62. 7th edition and 6th edition needed for full coverage.

Fleischer, M., *Glossary of Mineral Species*, published by the
Mineralogical Record every few years, Tucson, USA.

Hey, M. H., *Chemical Index to Minerals* (with two supplements),
London, Natural History Museum, 1962 & 1974.

O'Donoghue, M., ed., *Encyclopedia of Minerals and Gemstones*,
London, Orbis, 1976.

O'Donoghue, M., *The Literature of Mineralogy*, London, British
Library, 1986.

The literature of mineralogy is very large and professional help
should be sought before making serious use of it. Such help can
be obtained from the Science Reference and Information
Service of the British Library, London, England.

Acknowledgements

The author wishes to thank Dr Wendell E. Wilson and Dr Joel Arem for loaning many of the photographs illustrating this book. Grateful thanks are also extended to Martin Pulsford of the Natural History Museum, London, for arranging the supply of the remaining photographs.

Index

Bold type indicates illustrations